Moscow 1941

Hitler's first defeat

Moscow 1941

Hitler's first defeat

Robert Forczyk · Illustrated by Howard Gerrard

Series editor Lee Johnson

Transferred to digital print on demand 2010

First published 2006
4th impression 2008

Printed and bound by Cadmus Communications, USA

A CIP catalogue record for this book is available from the British Library

ISBN: 978 1 84603 017 8

Design by The Black Spot
Index by Alison Worthington
Maps by The Map Studio Ltd
3D bird's-eye views by The Black Spot
Battlescene illustrations by Howard Gerrard
Originated by United Graphic, Singapore
Typeset in Helvetica Neue and ITC New Baskerville

Dedication
This volume is dedicated to 2LT Mark J. Procopio, 3-172 IN, KIA in Ar-Ramadi 2 November 2005.

Acknowledgements
I wish to thank Mr Nik Cornish for the use of photographs from his large Eastern Front collection, as well as the staff at the
US National Archives (NARA).

Artist's note
Readers may care to note that the original paintings from which the colour plates in this book were prepared are available for
private sale. All reproduction copyright whatsoever is retained by the Publisher. Enquiries should be addressed to:

Howard Gerrard
11 Oaks Road
Tenterden
Kent
TN30 6RD
UK

The Publishers regret that they can enter into no correspondence upon this matter.

The Woodland Trust
Osprey Publishing is supporting the Woodland Trust, the UK's leading woodland conservation charity, by funding the
dedication of trees.

www.ospreypublishing.com

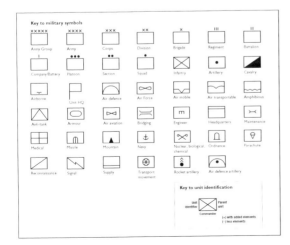

CONTENTS

ORIGINS OF THE CAMPAIGN   7

CHRONOLOGY   10

OPPOSING PLANS   11

German plans • Soviet plans

OPPOSING COMMANDERS   16

German commanders • Soviet commanders

OPPOSING FORCES   21

German forces • Soviet forces • Orders of battle

THE SURPRISE OFFENSIVE   30
30 SEPTEMBER – 15 OCTOBER 1941

Guderian routs Operational Group Ermakov • Fourth Panzer Army's attack
Third Panzer Army's attack • German infantry army attacks
The Soviet reaction • The Vyazma–Bryansk Pockets are formed
Guderian loses the initiative • The battle of the pockets and the pursuit
The Mozhaisk Line is breached

WAR OF ATTRITION   58
24 OCTOBER – 14 NOVEMBER 1941

Von Kluge fails to support Typhoon • Both sides prepare for one last effort

TYPHOON'S LAST GASP   70
15 NOVEMBER – 5 DECEMBER 1941

Rokossovsky under pressure • To the outskirts of Moscow
Guderian's last try for Tula

DESPERATE DAYS   84
5 – 15 DECEMBER 1941

German disaster in the Klin bulge • Guderian is routed

AFTERMATH   89

The weather factor • Conclusion

THE BATTLEFIELD TODAY   93

FURTHER READING   94

INDEX   95

STRATEGIC DISPOSITIONS ON THE EASTERN FRONT, 30 SEPTEMBER 1941

The Germans massed 54 per cent of their forces on the Eastern Front on the Moscow axis, including 16 of 18 panzer divisions in Russia. This was one of the rare occasions when the Germans enjoyed a numerical superiority in manpower, tanks and artillery.

EVENTS:
1. 15 September 1941, Leningrad encircled by German Army Group North (AGN) and Finns. German 18th Army shifts to defensive. 3rd Panzer Group is shifted to Army Group Centre (AGC).
2. 24 September 1941, the Kiev Pocket is crushed, allowing Army Group South (AGS) to shift forces eastward toward Kharkov. The Soviets struggle to re-establish a new South Front from remnants.
3. 24–28 September 1941, the German 11th Army begins its assault at Perekop to break into Crimea.
4. 26–29 September 1941, the Soviet Southwest Front counteroffensive against the German 11th Army fails with heavy losses.
5. 15 October 1941, the Soviet Coastal Army abandons Odessa and evacuates to reinforce the Crimea.

FINLAND

German Forces in Finland
(6 divisions
20 aircraft)

Finns

Rifle

BALTIC SEA

Reval

Lake Ladoga

Leningrad

Leningrad Front
ZHUKOV
(35 divisions
250 tanks
190 aircraft)

18

Novgorod

Novgorod Army Gp
(8 divisions
100 tanks)

Riga

1

KELLER
(250 aircraft)

North
VON LEEB
(26 divisions
200 tanks)

Pskov

16

North-western
(10 divisions
100 tanks)

Valdai Hills

Uncommitted Soviet Forces in Far East & Central Asia
(30+ divisions
500 tanks)

Uncommitted German Forces in Norway/Denmark
(6 divisions, 60 aircraft)

AGN
AGC

9

Rahev

6

PVO
(680 aircraft)

LRA
(360 bombers)

Gorki

Polotsk

3

Moscow

Vilna

Smolensk

KONEV
Western

Moscow Axis
(102 divisions
850 tanks
360 aircraft)

Minsk

Centre
VON BOCK
(71 divisions
1,300 tanks)

2
KESSELRING
(550 aircraft)

4

Reserve
BUDENNY

Kaluga

Tula

Stavka Reserves
(New units forming)
(20+ divisions
500 tanks)

Roslaul

4

Bryansk

Bryansk
YEREMENKO

Orel

Uncommitted German Forces in France/Holland
(28 divisions, 400 aircraft)

Gomel

2

Kursk

2

Uncommitted German Forces in Yugoslavia
(2 divisions)

Konotop

AGC
AGS

Kiev

6

South
RYABYSHEV
(25 divisions
250 tanks)

Kharkov

4
LOHR
(250 aircraft)

17

Kremenchug

South
VON RUNDSTEDT
(35 divisions
110 tanks)

1

Dneprotovsk

3 Rum

Southwest
TIMOSHENKO
(12 divisions
200 tanks)

Mariupol

Rostov

4 Rum

ROMANIA

Nikolayev

5

Odessa

Coastal
(2 divisions)

11

3

Uncommitted Soviet Forces on Turkish/Iranian borders
(12+ divisions
100 tanks)

51 Ind
KUZNETSOV
(9 divisions
100 tanks
330 aircraft)

Krasnodar

Sevastapol

BLACK SEA

Novorossiisk

CAUCASUS

AGC supply base
Front line, 30 Sept 1941
Army Group boundary

N

0   100 miles
0   200km

ORIGINS OF THE CAMPAIGN

Despite many indications of impending aggression, Hitler's invasion of the Soviet Union on 22 June 1941 caught the Red Army unprepared for war. Three German army groups – North, Centre and South – quickly broke through the Soviet border defences and plunged deep into the Soviet Union. Overhead, the Luftwaffe gained air superiority by inflicting crippling losses on the Soviet Air Force. While Army Group North overran the former Baltic States and Army Group South made slow progress towards Kiev, Army Group Centre was initially tasked with securing the vital Minsk–Orsha–Smolensk–Vitebsk corridor that would allow future exploitation towards Moscow. Hitler and the German OKH Staff anticipated that these series of heavy blows would lead to the rapid collapse of Soviet military power in 1941, requiring only limited subsequent mopping-up operations in 1942.

Army Group Centre, under Field Marshal von Bock, scored a major success in the first week of the campaign by encircling the bulk of the Soviet Western Front armies in the Bialystok–Minsk Pockets. In just seven days, Guderian's 2nd Panzer Group and Hoth's 3rd Panzer Group advanced 325km and linked up near Minsk to form these pockets. Although their reduction required a further ten days of hard fighting, the Soviet Western Front lost two-thirds of its strength, including over 300,000 prisoners and 2,500 tanks, in the first two weeks of the campaign. General Pavlov, the commander of the Western Front, was recalled to Moscow and executed.

While the Germans were busy reducing the Minsk Pocket, on 1 July 1941 Stalin ordered Marshal Timoshenko to take over command of the remnants of the Western Front and establish a new defensive line to protect Smolensk. Timoshenko had only a few days to cobble together a new front from escaped remnants of the border armies and hastily deployed Stavka reserves. When von Bock resumed Army Group Centre's advance in early July, he repeated the winning formula of double envelopment; again Hoth's Panzer Group bypassed the main Soviet defences and nearly linked up with Guderian's panzers on the far side of Smolensk on 15 July 1941. For the second time in a month, the bulk of the Soviet Western Front was virtually encircled. However, on this occasion, the Germans had greater difficulty in closing the final gap between the two panzer groups, partly because of Soviet resistance and partly because of competing tactical priorities. Guderian was negligent in making a major effort to close the gap, instead preferring to continue pushing east; on 17 July Guderian's panzers secured a bridgehead over the Desna River at Yelnya, only 300km from Moscow. Timoshenko was able to launch a counterattack on 23 July that penetrated the weak German cordon around Smolensk and allowed numerous Soviet troops to escape. An incensed von Bock ordered Guderian to cease all eastward movement and close the pocket but it was not until 27 July that the gap between Hoth's and Guderian's panzers was finally closed and the fighting in the pocket continued until 5 August. Soviet Western Front losses at Smolensk amounted to 310,000 prisoners and 3,200 tanks; Timoshenko's command had suffered 81 per cent losses in the two-month battle.

By mid-July, Army Group Centre had twice smashed clumsy Soviet defences and some German advance units were within 300km of Moscow. However, Soviet counterattacks on the southern flank of Army Group Centre were becoming serious and the advance of the other two German army groups was slowing down. Simultaneously, the supply situation of Army Group Centre was desperate and a respite was needed in order to prepare for further operations. On 19 July 1941, Hitler made his much-debated decision in Führer Directive 33 to shift effort away from the centre in order to energize the faltering flank drives. The directive stated that the destruction of Soviet forces around Kiev and Leningrad had priority and Army Group Centre was temporarily forced to detach both of its panzer groups to aid its neighbours. Believing that the Soviet Western Front was combat ineffective after the battle of Smolensk, Hitler ordered von Bock's reduced forces to continue 'advancing towards Moscow with infantry formations'. Hoth's panzers and one infantry army would support Army Group North's attacks, while Guderian's panzers and von Weichs' Second Army were sent to encircle Kiev. Essentially, von Kluge's Fourth Army was the only force still operating in the centre, and all its resources were absorbed in maintaining the Yelnya bridgehead. On 30 July 1941, Führer Directive 34 allowed Army Group Centre to temporarily shift to the defensive.

Many historians have harshly condemned Hitler's Kiev diversion, but the decision was militarily sound. The Soviet armies around Kiev were the most powerful forces at Stalin's disposal in 1941 and they could not simply be ignored; had von Bock pushed on towards Moscow without Kiev being taken, the 44 Soviet divisions in the Southwest Front would have almost certainly been used for a major counterattack against Guderian's flank. Without the intervention of Guderian's panzers, Army Group South might have been stopped cold outside Kiev, which in itself would have been a defeat. Furthermore, Hitler was fighting the campaign according to strategic priorities that were essentially sound: first, destroy the Soviet armies; second, seize key economic resource areas; and third, seize prestige objectives like Moscow or Leningrad. The diversion of Guderian's panzers resulted in the largest double envelopment in military history, with 616,000 Soviet troops lost in the Kiev operation. The Soviet Southwest Front was badly damaged and Army Group South raced to overrun much of the Ukraine and Crimea. By any measure, this was the greatest German

A German *Gefreiter* throws an M1939 hand grenade in a Russian village. Combat experience, excellent training and a proven doctrine gave the Wehrmacht's soldiers a huge advantage over the hastily raised Soviet conscripts of 1941. (NARA)

success of the campaign and the one that would take the Soviets the longest to reverse.

While Army Group Centre was temporarily on the defensive, the Soviets had used the respite to rebuild a new Western Front in order to protect Moscow. Instead of husbanding precious reserves, Stalin foolishly squandered them in a series of premature offensives. General Zhukov was given command of Stavka reserves and ordered to launch a major counterattack towards Smolensk and crush the weakened Army Group Centre. From 28 August until 8 September 1941, the Soviet Western Front launched a series of clumsy attacks that were unable to break the German defences but cost the Soviets heavily. The only major success was the elimination of the troublesome Yelnya salient, which the Germans abandoned on 6 September 1941 after suffering heavy losses. Zhukov's Yelnya counterattack was the first Soviet tactical victory of the war but the premature Soviet offensive had badly weakened the still-rebuilding Soviet Western Front. Further south, Stavka ordered the newly formed Bryansk Front under Yeremenko to attack Guderian's 2nd Panzer Group; Stalin ordered that, 'Guderian and his entire group must be smashed to smithereens.' Yeremenko's counteroffensive from 2 to 6 September 1941 was a disaster, costing another 100,000 Soviet casualties for no gain. Indeed, Stalin's premature late summer counterattacks were a major mistake that seriously weakened the Soviet centre.

By early September 1941, with the Kiev fighting approaching a climax, Hitler was relatively pleased with the course of Operation Barbarossa, except for the failure of Army Group North to seize Leningrad. Much of the Soviet army and air force appeared to have been destroyed, while key economic resource areas were within German grasp. Hitler considered shifting to a primarily defensive mode along much of the front once Kiev and the Ukraine had fallen, with Leningrad to succumb instead to a winter siege. Moscow, which Hitler never thought important, could be taken in the spring of 1942 by the revitalized German army. However, Hitler's mind was not fixed on the subject of Moscow and for once he allowed himself to be persuaded. A number of German generals, including von Bock, Kesselring, Guderian and Hoth, managed to convince Hitler that Moscow would be an easy objective to take given the heavy Soviet losses. While Hitler had hoped for a knockout blow against the USSR in 1941, he had in fact made plans for substantial follow-on operations in 1942, and was aware that the impending Soviet winter would seriously impede any renewed German offensive. Hitler was willing to consider an operational pause after the fall of Kiev, but von Bock and the other German military professionals convinced him that taking Moscow was both achievable and worth the risk.

CHRONOLOGY

1941

4 August	Hitler conference at Army Group Centre: von Bock, Guderian and Hoth press Hitler to advance on Moscow. Hitler says that Leningrad, the Ukraine and the Crimea are the main objectives.
5 August	The battle of the Smolensk Pocket ends.
21 August	Führer Directive 34 orders main effort in south; Moscow is a secondary objective.
30 August	Zhukov begins counterattack to retake Yelnya salient.
6 September	Führer Directive Number 35 makes Moscow the objective. Army Group Centre withdraws Fourth Army from Yelnya salient.
30 September	Guderian's 2nd Panzer Group starts Typhoon by attacking the Soviet Bryansk Front.
2 October	3rd and 4th Panzer Groups begin main assault of Operation Typhoon.
3 October	Stavka airlifts the 5th Airborne Corps into Orel, but the city falls to 2nd Panzer Group. Third Panzer Army seizes bridge over Dnepr River at Kholm.
4–5 October	Von Kluge's Fourth Army crushes the Soviet armies around Yelnya.
5 October	Panzer Groups renamed Panzer Armies. Stavka permits Western Front to pull back towards Vyazma.
6 October	Russian counterattack near Mtensk. Second Panzer Army captures Bryansk.
7 October	Germans capture Vyazma, trapping elements of four Soviet armies.
8–9 October	Three Soviet armies are isolated around Bryansk.
9 October	SS Reich Division captures Gzhatsk.
10 October	Zhukov takes command of Western Front. Second Panzer Army takes Mtensk.
12 October	Organized resistance in the Bryansk Pocket ends. German XIII Corps captures Kaluga.
13 October	Rzhev captured by Third Panzer Army.
14 October	Kalinin is captured by Third Panzer Army.
15–17 October	Battle of Borodino.
15 October	Soviet Government begins evacuating Moscow.
18 October	Germans capture Mozhaisk.
19–29 October	Konev counterattacks German forces in Kalinin.
22–23 October	Guderian's Second Panzer Army crosses Zusha River at Mtensk.
27 October	Volokolamsk is captured.
28–29 October	Guderian's first attempt to storm Tula fails.
3–13 November	Soviet 3rd Army attacks Guderian's right flank at Teploye.
15–18 November	Third and Fourth Panzer Armies begin second phase of Typhoon.
23 November	Third Panzer Army captures Klin.
27 November	Istra falls to Fourth Panzer Army.
24 November	Second Panzer Army begins its final offensive.
27 November	Third Panzer Army crosses Moskva–Volga canal at Yakhroma.
30 November	2nd Panzer Division captures Krasnaya Polyana.
1 December	German Fourth Army achieves break through on Nara River, but the offensive is checked after less than 48 hours.
2-4 December	Guderian's last bid to encircle Tula fails.
4-5 December	Operation Typhoon is suspended. Extreme cold weather arrives.
5 December	Konev's Kalinin Front begins the Winter Counteroffensive.
6 December	Zhukov's Western Front launches major counteroffensive against all three German panzer armies.
10 December	German XXXIV Corps is encircled near Livny by Timoshenko's Southwest Front.
11 December	Soviets recapture Istra and Solnechnogorsk.
15 December	Third Panzer Army abandons Klin.

OPPOSING PLANS

GERMAN PLANS

Since the start of planning for Operation Barbarossa, Hitler and the OKW Staff had disagreed on the relative importance of Moscow as a campaign objective. Hitler was ambivalent about Moscow, preferring the destruction of Soviet field armies before diverting resources to seize prestige targets, but the OKW staff consistently advocated the Soviet capital as a worthwhile objective. The original Barbarossa plan was a compromise between Hitler and the OKW, which stated that 'the capture of this city [Moscow] would be a decisive victory both from the political and from the economic point of view; it would involve, moreover, the neutralization of the most vital Russian rail centre.' However, Hitler ordered that Moscow would only be captured after the destruction of the bulk of the Soviet armies and the occupation of Leningrad. Once Barbarossa started, Hitler remained focused on smashing one Soviet army after another and Moscow was not on his list of priorities.

Yet in the Addendum to Führer Directive 34, issued on 12 August 1941, Field Marshal Wilhelm Keitel, head of the OKW, inserted Moscow as a future priority objective by stating that:

> After the threatening situation on the flanks has been completely elim-
> inated and the panzer groups have been refitted conditions will be
> conducive for an offensive ... across a broad front against the large
> enemy forces concentrated for the defence of Moscow. The aim of this
> offensive is to capture the enemy's entire complex of state economic and
> communications centres in the Moscow region before the onset of winter,
> by doing so, depriving him of the capability for restoring his destroyed
> armed forces and smashing the functioning of state control apparatus.

Colonel General Franz Halder (Chief of the OKH), von Bock and Guderian attempted to redirect the German primary focus back to the centre, away from the southern front. An irritated Hitler responded on 21 August 1941 with an order to both staffs:

> The OKH's 18 August considerations regarding the further conduct
> of operations in the East do not agree with my intentions. I order:
> the most important missions before the onset of winter are to seize the
> Crimea and the industrial and coal regions of the Don, deprive the
> Russians of the opportunity to obtain oil from the Caucasus and, in
> the north, to encircle Leningrad and link up with the Finns rather
> than capture Moscow.

Hitler met with von Bock at Army Group Centre's headquarters on 4 August 1941. Although von Bock pressed for an immediate advance on Moscow, Hitler directed that the economic resources of the Ukraine were a greater strategic priority. (NARA)

Two weeks later, the strategic picture changed with German successes in the south and north, coupled with the disastrous Soviet counterattacks in the centre. Hitler, misled by faulty and overly optimistic German intelligence estimates, concluded that the entire Soviet front was tottering and that one more catastrophe would lead to a complete collapse. In Führer Directive 35, dated 6 September, Hitler stated that German success on the flanks had created the 'prerequisites for conducting a decisive operation against Army Group Timoshenko, which is conducting unsuccessful offensive operations on Army Group Centre's front. It must be destroyed decisively before the onset of winter.' However, it is important to note that Hitler ordered the destruction of the Soviet Western Front, not the capture of Moscow. Indeed, the directive states that, 'after destroying the main mass of Timoshenko's group of forces in this decisive encirclement and destruction operation, Army Group Centre is to begin pursuing enemy forces *along* the Moscow axis' but the order specified maintaining contact with the adjoining army groups rather than seizure of the capital. Hitler directed Army Group Centre to destroy Timoshenko's armies east of Smolensk by means of a double envelopment, but pursuit operations were left ambiguous.

The OKH and Army Group Centre staffs took Hitler's guidance and developed the operational plan for Operation Typhoon, one of the largest German offensive operations of the war. Initially, von Bock hoped to begin the Typhoon offensive in mid-September but delays in redeploying the panzer groups, rainy weather and logistical problems resulted in its being delayed several times. Although Hitler's directive had only ordered the commitment of the 3rd and 4th Panzer Groups to encircle the Soviet armies around Vyazma, on his own initiative von Bock decided to add Guderian's depleted 2nd Panzer Group to create another encirclement around Bryansk and thereby rip open the entire Soviet central front. Guderian's panzers, which were the furthest from Moscow, were allowed to attack on 30 September 1941 but the main German attack would commence on 2 October. At the beginning of Typhoon, the actual method of capturing Moscow was not specified but either envelopment by the two flanking panzer groups or a *coup de main* up the centre was assumed.

The Germans massed six armies for Typhoon, with a total of 15 panzer, eight motorized and 47 infantry divisions. For the first time in the campaign in the Soviet Union, the Germans enjoyed both quantitative and qualitative superiority; Army Group Centre had an overall 1.5:1 superiority in manpower, 1.7:1 in tanks, 1.8:1 in artillery and 2.1:1 in aircraft. Nevertheless, Typhoon was a gamble since the Germans lacked the logistic resources for another protracted offensive and adverse weather would soon impact operational mobility. Indeed, Army Group Centre had to win quickly or not at all.

SOVIET PLANS

The disagreements between Hitler and the OKH staff over the importance of Moscow actually worked to Germany's advantage, since Soviet intelligence was able to obtain some information about German intentions through as-yet-unrevealed sources.

Soviet human intelligence was effective but misleading, since it revealed only what the OKH, not Hitler, intended. Thus after the battle of Smolensk, when the OKH wanted to press on towards Moscow, Stalin was informed that the capital was the main objective and he reinforced the shaky Western Front. Hitler's diversion towards Kiev caught the Soviets by surprise and Stalin began to doubt Soviet intelligence, preferring to rely on his dictatorial intuition. After the battle of Kiev, Stalin assumed that it was too late in the season for a major drive on Moscow, so he decided to send the bulk of Stavka reserves to reinforce the south-west and Leningrad, weakening the relatively quiet central sector.

The Soviet defences around Moscow consisted of the Western Front (Konev), the Reserve Front (Budenny) and the Bryansk Front (Yeremenko). All three fronts had actually been counterattacking during August–September and Stavka did not order the Western Front to assume a defensive posture until 10 September. While Stavka ordered a defence-in-depth with powerful mobile reserves, this was not possible due to the heavy losses in the recent futile counterattacks. Even without the heavy armour losses in the Smolensk fighting, the lack of sufficient motor transport, artillery and trained reserves severely limited Soviet options. On the Bryansk Front, Yeremenko requested permission to conduct a mobile defence, but was denied by Shaposhnikov since Stalin was becoming less willing to trade space for time as the German spearheads penetrated deeper into the Soviet Union. Indeed, the Soviet Army was so offensively oriented in 1941 that it spent more time planning tactical attacks than operational-level defence.

Soviet dispositions on the Moscow axis were clumsy, with two of the six armies of the Reserve Front occupying the front between the Western and Bryansk Fronts. German tactical intelligence had detected the frontal boundaries in close proximity and the 4th Panzer Group was positioned to exploit the seam between the Reserve Front and the Bryansk Front. Too many of the Soviet forces were deployed close behind the front in anticipation of a forthcoming offensive, which meant, however, that much of the relatively immobile artillery would be lost in the event of further retreats. Dovator's Cavalry Group, the only significant mobile reserve belonging to the Western Front, was awkwardly deployed right

Marshal Boris Shaposhnikov, Soviet Chief of General Staff. During Typhoon, Shaposhnikov played a major role in gathering reinforcements from the vast Soviet hinterland and he planned the Winter Counteroffensive. (David Glantz)

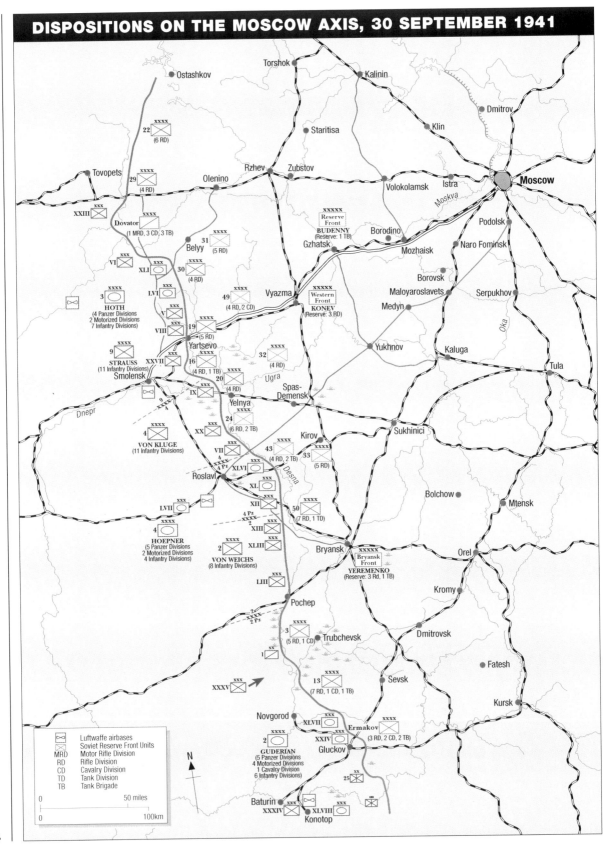

Torshok

Ostashkov

Kalinin

Dmitrov

22 XXXX (6 RD)

Staritsa

Klin

Tovopets

29 XXXX (4 RD)

Olenino

Rzhev

Zubstov

Volokolamsk

Istra

Moskva

Moscow

XXIII XXX

Dovator (1 MRD, 3 CD, 3 TB)

31 XXXX (5 RD)

Belyy

Reserve Front
BUDENNY
(Reserve: 1 TB) XXXXX

Borodino

Podolsk

Naro Fominsk

VI XXX

XLI XXX

30 XXXX (4 RD)

Gzhatsk

Mozhaisk

Borovsk

Serpukhov

3 HOTH
(4 Panzer Divisions
2 Motorized Divisions
7 Infantry Divisions) XXXX

LVI XXX

V XXX

49 XXXX (4 RD, 2 CD)

Vyazma

Western Front
KONEV
(Reserve: 3 RD) XXXXX

Maloyaroslavets

Medyn

VIII XXX

19 XXXX (5 RD)

Yartsevo

32 XXXX (4 RD)

Yukhnov

Kaluga

Tula

9 STRAUSS
(11 Infantry Divisions) XXXX

XXVII XXX

16 XXXX (4 RD, 1 TB)

Smolensk

IX XXX

20 XXXX (4 RD)

Ugra

Spas-
Demensk

Sukhinici

Dnepr

Yelnya

24 XXXX (6 RD, 2 TB)

Kirov

4 XXXX

VON KLUGE
(11 Infantry Divisions)

VII XXX

43 XXXX (4 RD, 2 TB)

33 XXXX (5 RD)

XX XXX

4 Pz XXXX

XLVI XXX

Desna

Roslavl

XL XXX

Bolchow

Mtensk

LVII XXX

XII XXX

50 XXXX (7 RD, 1 TD)

4 Pz XXXX 2

XIII XXX

4 HOEPNER
(5 Panzer Divisions
2 Motorized Divisions
4 Infantry Divisions) XXXX

2 XXXX

XLIII XXX

Bryansk

Bryansk
Front
YEREMENKO
(Reserve: 3 Rd, 1 TB) XXXXX

Orel

VON WEICHS
(8 Infantry Divisions)

LIII XXX

Kromy

2 Pz XXXX 2

Pochep

Dmitrovsk

3 XXXX (5 RD, 1 CD)

Trubchevsk

1 XX

Fatesh

XXXV XXX

13 XXXX (7 RD, 1 CD, 1 TB)

Sevsk

Kursk

Novgorod

XLVII XXX

Ermakov XXXX (3 RD, 2 CD, 2 TB)

2 XXXX

XXIV XXX

Gluckov

GUDERIAN
(5 Panzer Divisions
4 Motorized Divisions
1 Cavalry Division
6 Infantry Divisions)

25 XX

N

XXXIV XXX

XLVIII XXX

Baturin

Konotop

⋈	Luftwaffe airbases
⊠	Soviet Reserve Front Units
MRD	Motor Rifle Division
RD	Rifle Division
CD	Cavalry Division
TD	Tank Division
TB	Tank Brigade

0 ———— 50 miles

0 ———— 100km

14

behind the front and in a poor position to redeploy in the event of a German threat elsewhere.

In mid-July 1941, Stavka had ordered construction of a series of defensive lines around Moscow, consisting of anti-tank ditches, mines and concrete or log bunkers. The outermost line was west of Vyazma, which is where the front stabilized after the battle of Smolensk. The inner line was centred on Mozhaisk, on the direct route into Moscow, with other fortified areas around Volokolamsk, Maloyaroslavets and Kaluga. Although the Soviets mobilized large numbers of civilians to assist military engineers in constructing the defensive lines, these positions were less than half complete at the start of Typhoon. The four main fortified areas had 296 concrete bunkers, 538 log or earth bunkers and 170km of anti-tank ditches, but very few troops actually manned the defences.

Having misjudged the German intention to invade and the German decision to divert to Kiev – both of which cost the Soviet Union dearly – Stalin capped his near-fatal mistakes of 1941 with the erroneous assumption that the Germans would not attack towards Moscow so late in the season. Soviet intelligence failed to detect the regrouping of German forces under Army Group Centre and believed that the main effort would remain in the south. When Typhoon opened, Stavka was planning further offensives against Army Group Centre in the fall, not expecting a desperate defence of the capital.

OPPOSING COMMANDERS

GERMAN COMMANDERS

The German officers who led Operation Typhoon were an extremely professional and experienced group of leaders. However, not all of them were comfortable with the new blitzkrieg doctrine and many were resentful of the Nazi regime. Furthermore, many of the senior German commanders were too old to stand up to the physical and mental demands of protracted, high-intensity warfare.

Field Marshal Fedor von Bock had been the commander of Army Group Centre since June 1941. The 60-year-old von Bock was one of the most experienced large-formation commanders in the Wehrmacht of 1941, having commanded Army Group North in Poland in 1939 and Army Group B in Belgium and Holland in 1940. Von Bock was a conservative commander, willing to adapt to the new blitzkrieg doctrine but uncomfortable with non-linear or unconventional concepts of warfare. Most of all, von Bock was out of touch with what his troops were enduring as the weather worsened; at one point he visited a forward regimental command post and was surprised to find 'that the staff operates in a most primitive manner in foxholes'. Von Bock spent a great deal of time in his well-equipped headquarters train near Smolensk – the mud and snow was mostly theoretical to him. Von Bock was also an arrogant leader who got along poorly with most of his army commanders, but was overly tolerant of insubordination from von Kluge and Guderian. Once Operation Typhoon began to unwind, it was von Bock who pushed to keep the offensive going lest he fall short of his objective.

Colonel General Heinz Guderian, commander of 2nd Panzer Group since November 1940. Guderian was trained as a signal and transportation officer and his interest in technology led to his interest in mechanization. Guderian was the innovator who designed and built Germany's armoured forces and he commanded one of the first panzer divisions in 1935. In 1939–40, Guderian's XIX Corps spearheaded the victories in Poland and France. At the start of Operation Barbarossa, Guderian was given command of the 2nd Panzer Group, which achieved major victories at Minsk, Smolensk and Kiev in the first three months of the campaign. By the start of Typhoon, the 53-year-old Guderian was the most experienced armour commander on earth, but he was also mentally exhausted and resentful of his chain of command. Guderian was a difficult subordinate – often ignoring von Bock's orders when he disagreed with them – and he was barely on speaking terms with von Kluge.

Colonel General Erich Hoepner, commander of 4th Panzer Group since 15 February 1941. Hoepner was a cavalry officer turned panzer expert. At the start of the war Hoepner was commander of XVI Corps in Poland and France. In Operation Barbarossa, Hoepner led the 4th

Colonel General Heinz Guderian, commander of 2nd Panzer Group. Although Guderian had led the panzer spearheads to victory in Poland, France and the early days of Barbarossa, he was exhausted and quarrelsome by the start of Typhoon. (NARA)

Colonel General Hans Georg Reinhardt took over command of Third Panzer Army on 5 October 1941. Reinhardt was one of the most experienced German panzer leaders in the Wehrmacht at the start of Typhoon. (NARA)

Panzer Group in the advance upon Leningrad. Hoepner was an energetic and aggressive panzer leader, but a difficult subordinate. Early in the war, Hoepner was aware of, if not involved in, the conspiracy against Hitler, and his anti-Nazi opinions made him a convenient scapegoat when Typhoon failed.

Colonel General Hans Georg Reinhardt took command of Third Panzer Army from Colonel General Hermann Hoth on 5 October 1941. Reinhardt commanded the 4th Panzer Division in the 1939 Polish campaign, where his division suffered heavy losses on the outskirts of Warsaw. Afterwards, Reinhardt commanded XLI Corps in France in 1940, Yugoslavia in 1941 and then the advance to Leningrad in 1941.

Field Marshal Günther von Kluge was commander of Fourth Army since the start of the war in 1939, and he led it in Poland, France and the invasion of the USSR. The 58-year-old von Kluge was a talented professional but he did not get along with his peers, particularly Guderian. Operationally, von Kluge was an old-style set-piece commander who didn't like advancing until he had dealt with all enemy pockets and logistical problems. Von Kluge's failure to attack on the Nara River in November 1941 with the rest of Army Group Centre helped to doom Typhoon's final efforts. Von Kluge was also disloyal to von Bock as well as being involved in the conspiracy to overthrow Hitler.

Colonel General Adolf Strauss was commander of Ninth Army since 29 May 1940. Strauss commanded II Corps in Poland in 1939. The 62-year-old Strauss was not in good health after three months of active campaigning in Barbarossa. Strauss failed to understand the importance of having his infantry catch up with the panzer spearheads and tended to use his reserves to settle local actions, rather than reinforce the main effort.

Colonel General Maximilian Von Weichs was commander of Second Army since October 1939. Weichs was a Bavarian cavalryman and General Staff-trained officer. Weichs admired Hitler for rebuilding the German army and in 1935 Weichs was given command of the newly raised 1st Panzer Division. During the Polish Campaign, von Weichs commanded XIII Corps but he was only involved in mopping-up operations during the 1940 French campaign. In Yugoslavia, von Weichs' Second Army formed the main effort and due to this diversion he arrived in the USSR after the

start of Operation Barbarossa. During Typhoon, the 60-year-old Weichs was plagued by ill health. Weichs was unusual also in maintaining Hitler's respect to the end of the war.

Most of the German panzer corps commanders were in their mid-fifties and came from cavalry backgrounds.[1] **General Leo Baron Geyr von Schweppenburg**, commander of XXIV Panzer Corps since February 1940, had previously commanded the 3rd Panzer Division in Poland. **General Georg Stumme**, commander of the XL Panzer Corps since February 1940, had led the 2nd Light Division in Poland in 1939. **General Joachim Lemelsen**, commander of XLVII Panzer Corps since November 1940, had commanded the 29th Motorized Division in Poland and the 5th Panzer Division in France in 1940. One of the most unique corps commanders was **Colonel General Walther Model**, who took command of XLI Panzer Corps just two days before the start of Typhoon. Model was an infantryman who served as a staff officer during the Polish and French campaigns and did not get his first major command – 3rd Panzer Division – until November 1940. Model was particularly unusual for a senior Wehrmacht officer in that he was a Nazi party member and extremely loyal to Hitler. Model was not constrained by his staff training; his Nazi ideology and ambition led him to believe that the impossible could be achieved through hard work and fanaticism – which made him a very attractive leader to Hitler. Model was one of the few German generals to enhance their careers during Typhoon and he became a prototype for the late-war German commander.

The German spearheads were led by a new generation of aggressive field commanders that would prove themselves on the Eastern Front and quickly rise to high command. **Colonel Heinrich Eberbach**, commander of the 5th Panzer Brigade/4th Panzer Division, led Guderian's spearhead. **Colonel Hasso von Manteuffel**, commander of 6th Rifle Regiment/7th Panzer Division, led Reinhardt's spearhead.

SOVIET COMMANDERS

The Soviet senior officers involved in defending Moscow were generally less experienced than their German counterparts but they were typically five to ten years younger, which made them better able to withstand the arduous three-month Typhoon campaign. The proportion of cavalry officers in dominant positions was also very high. Unlike the Wehrmacht officer corps, the Soviet officers were all politically reliable, since the purges of the 1930s had instilled a deep fear of anti-regime attitudes in the survivors.

Marshal Boris Shaposhnikov, Soviet Chief of General Staff, was a former Tsarist officer who was trained in the General Staff Academy before World War I and rose to command a grenadier regiment by 1917. When the Revolution came, Shaposhnikov served as a key staff officer who helped to plan most of the Red Army's operations, and then played a major role in postwar reorganization. Shaposhnikov was a talented staff officer and his General Staff was responsible for concentrating troops to defend the capital during Typhoon and planning the counteroffensive.

General Georgi Zhukov took command of the Western Front on 10 October 1941 when Konev was relieved. The 44-year-old Zhukov was

ABOVE **General Georgi Zhukov assumed command of the Western Front on 10 October 1941. Zhukov was a bold, aggressive commander who did not buckle in a crisis, but he tended to squander the lives of his troops in sloppy, amateurish attacks in order to satisfy Stalin's demands for prompt results. (David Glantz)**

BOTTOM **Colonel General Ivan Konev, commander of the Soviet Western Front at the start of Typhoon. When the bulk of his command was annihilated, Stalin relieved him and ordered his execution – but Zhukov was able to change the dictator's mind and get Konev re-instated as commander of the new Kalinin Front. (NARA)**

Major General Konstantin Rokossovsky was commander of the Soviet 16th Army. During Typhoon, Rokossovsky's army had to bear the brunt of the final German advance on Moscow and his relationship with Zhukov soured when he began to question his 'die in place' orders. (NARA)

Lieutenant General Ivan Boldin, Commander of the 50th Army. Boldin had escaped from the Minsk Pocket in July 1941 and the Vyazma Pocket in October 1941. Boldin's dogged defence of Tula and persistent counter-attacks against Guderian's left flank doomed the German southern pincer against Moscow. (David Glantz)

conscripted into the Tsarist Army in 1915. During the Russian Civil War he joined the Red Army and rose to command a cavalry regiment. Zhukov was lucky in surviving the Stalinist purges and then rose to prominence when he defeated the Japanese at Nomonhan in 1939. At the start of Barbarossa, Zhukov was director of Stavka and he urged Stalin to withdraw from Kiev in July 1941 but was instead relieved on 30 July and sent to command the Reserve Front. In August 1941, Zhukov went as Stavka representative to the Western Front where he ordered the partially successful counterattacks against the German spearheads near Smolensk, but his counterattack at Yelnya in September 1941 was a costly success. On 10 September, Zhukov was dispatched to shore up Leningrad's defences. Zhukov played the role of fireman in the Soviet army – moving from crisis to crisis, but his reputation as 'the general who never lost a battle' is a product of communist propaganda. Zhukov was an aggressive operational commander who was undaunted by losses, but his attacks were often poorly coordinated and he tended to squander his reserves in many small division-level attacks rather than massing for decisive results. Zhukov was often very brutal with subordinates but he was also fearful of Stalin's wrath in the event of failure.

Lieutenant General Ivan Konev took command of the Western Front on 12 September 1941. Konev was drafted into the Tsarist Army and later switched to the Reds but he saw little action in the period 1916–19. He graduated from the Frunze Military Academy in 1926 and served in the Far East in 1937–41. At the start of Barbarossa, Konev was commanding Nineteenth Army on the Western Front and fought at Vitebsk. Stalin held Konev personally responsible for the Vyazma–Bryansk encirclements and it was Zhukov who saved him from execution. On 17 October, Konev was given command of the new Kalinin Front. Konev was an aggressive operational commander who favoured set-piece battles with massed armour and artillery, but in 1941 he had to make do with depleted and untrained forces that were ill suited to his methods.

Lieutenant General Andrei Yeremenko was the 49-year-old commander of the Bryansk Front since 16 August 1941. Like Zhukov, Yeremenko was drafted into the Tsarist Army and eventually switched to the Red cavalry. He commanded a cavalry corps during the occupation of eastern Poland in 1939 and was an army commander in the Far East at the start of Barbarossa. Yeremenko was quickly recalled to Moscow and he helped to rebuild the shattered Western Front in July 1941.

Major General Konstantin Rokossovsky was the commander of 16th Army since late September 1941. Like Zhukov and Yeremenko, Rokossovsky enlisted in the Tsarist Army and then switched to the Red cavalry during the Russian Civil War. He was arrested during the purges in 1937 and spent 31 months in prison. He was eventually re-instated and given command of the partly formed 9th Mechanized Corps in October 1940. At the start of Barbarossa, Rokossovsky led his corps in an unsuccessful counterattack near Rovno in the Ukraine on 25 June. Afterwards, he was transferred to the Smolensk area on 14 July and took command of an ad hoc corps. Rokossovsky eventually became one of the best Soviet wartime generals, but in 1941 he was still learning to command large-scale forces. During Typhoon, Rokossovsky's previously

Major General Dmitri Lelyushenko was the most effective Soviet tactical commander during Typhoon. He played a major role in frustrating German plans at Mtensk and Borodino, and then routed Reinhardt's Third Panzer Army in the battle of the Klin Bulge. (David Glantz)

close relationship with Zhukov soured because he questioned repeated orders for his army to die in place.

Lieutenant General Ivan V. Boldin was the Deputy Commander of the Western Front from June to October 1941 and was given command of the 50th Army at Tula on 22 November. In 1939, Boldin commanded an army-sized mechanized cavalry group in the invasion of Poland. As deputy Western Front commander, he led a futile counterattack west of Minsk and succeeded in breaking out of the pocket with 1,600 troops. Boldin had modest military talents but was tenacious in the defence.

Major General Dmitri Danilovich Lelyushenko was the commander of 1 Guard Corps from 1 to 10 October 1941, which was organized at Mtensk to block Guderian's advance. From 11 to 16 October, Lelyushenko commanded 5th Army that was formed to hold the Mozhaisk Line, until he was badly wounded at the battle of Borodino. Lelyushenko returned on 17 November to command 30th Army's desperate defence of Klin. Lelyushenko was the most important operational Soviet commander in Typhoon, serving to frustrate the German timetable at three critical points. Lelyushenko started his career in the Red cavalry during the Russian Civil War and commanded a tank brigade in the invasion of Poland in 1939. He was also one of the very few officers who made a name for himself in the Russo-Finnish War, where he breached the Finnish Mannerheim Line. At the start of Barbarossa, Lelyushenko's 21st Mechanized Corps was decimated and unable to stop von Manstein's advance through the Baltic States. In late 1941, Lelyushenko was the Soviet Union's best operational-level armour leader.

Despite a string of defeats in the summer of 1941, the Red Army also had several rising stars at brigade level. **Colonel Mikhail E. Katukov** was probably the best Soviet tactical armour leader in late 1941. Katukov served in the Red cavalry then switched to the new tank corps in 1932. He led the 20th Tank Division in the Ukraine at the start of Barbarossa, but after this unit was destroyed he was sent to Stalingrad to take command of the 4th Tank Brigade, equipped with T-34 tanks. Katukov was able to learn from German methods and he was able to train his unit to a much higher standard than most Soviet tank units in 1941. Katukov and his 4th Tank Brigade was the best Soviet armour unit to face Typhoon. **Colonel Pavel A. Rotmistrov** was a skilled armour officer and military intellectual, who led the 8th Tank Brigade in the fighting around Kalinin.

1 German nomenclature about the panzer corps was in a state of flux at the time of Typhoon. XL, XLVI, XLVII, XLVIII and LVI were officially panzer corps, and XXIV was listed as a panzer corps in 2nd Panzer Group records. XLI and LVII Corps did not receive the designation 'Panzer Corps' until the summer of 1942 and during Typhoon were identified as either 'Army Corps' or 'Motorized Corps'. To avoid confusion, I identify all eight armoured corps in Army Group Centre during Typhoon as 'Panzer Corps'. Panzer groups were redesignated panzer armies on 5 October 1941, meaning that their nomenclature changed during the first week of Typhoon. To avoid confusion, they will be called panzer groups prior to Typhoon, but panzer armies once Typhoon starts.

OPPOSING FORCES

GERMAN FORCES

The German Army in September 1941 was at the height of its military prowess, comprising a well-trained and combat-experienced force that was led by competent military professionals. While the German troops and their leaders had begun to appreciate the tenacity of their Soviet opponents in the battle of Smolensk, the string of impressive victories reinforced the Wehrmacht's belief in its innate superiority over their foes. At the cutting edge of Operation Typhoon were the panzer corps, which combined armour, motorized infantry, motorized artillery, pioneers and motorized reconnaissance into a lethal combined-arms team. Combat losses and mechanical breakdowns had worn down the panzer divisions after three months of continuous fighting in the USSR, but Guderian's divisions still had 50 per cent or more of their tanks and equipment at the start of Typhoon, while Reinhardt's divisions had close to 80 per cent strength. Two panzer divisions – the 2nd and 5th – had just arrived at the front after re-equipping in France and started Typhoon at full strength in equipment and manpower. These divisions were both assigned to the Fourth Panzer Army. However, many of the German tanks were badly in need of depot-level repairs due to worn-out engines and transmissions. Hitler had ordered that all tank engine production should go for new vehicle construction rather than spares for existing units, and Army Group Centre received only 350 tank engines just prior to Typhoon to bring some vehicles back into service.

By the third month of Barbarossa, the Ostheer's infantry divisions were exhausted after a series of endless marches and pocket-reduction battles. Most divisions had 75–80 per cent strength in personnel but material losses had been fairly light. Although still armed with the outdated Pak 36 37mm anti-tank gun, the German infantry had begun to receive the better Pak 38 50mm anti-tank gun. The Germans were also beginning to experiment with self-propelled anti-tank guns and the 8th and 28th Infantry Divisions in Ninth Army each received ten self-propelled 88mm guns on an SdKfz 8 halftrack chassis. Furthermore, Army Group Centre had 14 assault-gun battalions with about 350 StuG IIIs, which gave the infantry corps more firepower.

Army Group Centre's artillery played an important role in Typhoon. Artillery was still necessary to achieve breakthroughs against fixed defences and was also critical in defeating the all-too-frequent Soviet counterattacks. Indeed, the German divisional artillery regiment provided about 60 per cent of the firepower in that formation and as infantry losses mounted, the Germans became increasingly reliant on their artillery. At the start of Typhoon, Army Group Centre had amassed about 4,000 heavy calibre weapons (including 2,300 105mm, 1,000

A German 37mm Pak 36 anti-tank gun destroyed by Soviet tanks, its dead crew and Soviet infantrymen lying nearby. Each German division typically had 45 37mm guns in October 1941, as well as nine of the better 50mm Pak 38 guns. (NARA)

150mm, 184 210mm guns and 270 *Nebelwerfer* rocket launchers). Yet only one-third of the German artillery was motorized, the rest being horse-drawn just as it was in 1918. While German artillery losses thus far in Barbarossa had been light, its effectiveness was plagued by mobility problems caused by the shortage of trucks and Russia's primitive roads. Thousands of trucks and horses had been lost before Typhoon even started, leaving the German artillery with a narrow margin of mobility.

The other vital part of the combined-arms team was Luftwaffe ground support. The Luftwaffe had been providing excellent close air support to the army for the first three months of Barbarossa but by October heavy losses and lack of adequate maintenance at forward airstrips had reduced this formidable force. For Typhoon, Kesselring's Luftflotte 2 had about 549 aircraft operational – approximately 230 bombers (He 111, Do 17 and Ju 88) in 13 *Kampfgruppen*, 190 fighters (Bf 109) in nine *Jagdgruppen* and about 120 ground attack aircraft (Ju 87 Stuka and Bf 110) in eight groups. General von Richthofen's VIII Fliegerkorps had developed into the premier close air support organization in the Luftwaffe and was a major combat multiplier for the Germans. The

The German PzKpfw IVE medium tank, introduced in December 1939, incorporated bolt-on armour plates. At the start of Typhoon, Army Group Centre had about 200 PzKpfw IV tanks. The low-velocity 75mm L/24 howitzer on the PzKpfw IVE was designed more for infantry support than the anti-tank role. (Author's collection)

A German 210mm howitzer firing at night. Army Group Centre had 15 heavy artillery battalions supporting Typhoon. This artillery piece was one of the most powerful in the Wehrmacht's arsenal and had a maximum range of 16,700m. (Nik Cornish at Stavka)

Luftwaffe also had detachments from II Flak Corps, equipped with the powerful 88mm Flak 36 dual-purpose gun, attached to each of the panzer groups.

Army Group Centre's main weakness was logistics, which had been parlous from the beginning of the campaign. Only two *Eisenbahn* regiments for repairing captured Soviet rail lines were assigned to support Army Group Centre and they soon proved to be inadequately manned, trained and equipped. While the *Eisenbahn* units were capable of regauging up to 20km of the Soviet broad-gauge rail lines per day, they also had to rebuild damaged bridges and repair various train facilities. Even once repaired, the rail lines supporting Army Group Centre were operating far below capacity; instead of receiving 30 trains with about 450 tons of supply each per day, Army Group Centre typically received only 12–20 in the autumn of 1941. Gross inefficiency in the German logistical pipeline in Poland, caused by competing commanders in charge of railway and logistic depots, further contributed to bottlenecks that starved Army Group Centre of vital material. A classic example of these bottlenecks was the issue of winter clothing; contrary to popular myth, Hitler had not forbidden the issuing of winter clothing. However, due to the limited rail capacity of the lines going into occupied Russia, winter clothing was assigned a much lower priority than fuel or ammunition. Much of the clothing was stockpiled in depots in Poland awaiting transport.

At the start of Typhoon, Army Group Centre had four main railheads supplying its six armies: Nevel, Smolensk, Roslavl and Gomel. The German logistic pipeline could operate no more than 100km from these railheads and relied primarily on trucks to bring supplies up to the forward units. Army Group Centre had one *Grosstransportraum* or motor transport regiment, with about 1,500 vehicles and a capacity of 6,500 tons, to transport supplies to the corps, which then used organic transport to supply their own divisions. Luftflotte 2 also had three transport groups with Ju 52 transport planes capable of carrying about 200 tons that could also provide air resupply to the army if necessary. However, Army Group Centre was experiencing fuel and ammunition shortages even before the onset of bad weather because of the inability to bring forward sufficient

quantities of supplies from the railheads; Army Group Centre's 70 divisions required in excess of 13,000 tons of supply per day but the truck and horse transport columns were incapable of filling more than 65 per cent of this requirement. As the distance from the railheads to the front line increased and inclement weather arrived, German supply capabilities diminished to less than one-third of requirements.

To make matters even worse, the Wehrmacht was running dangerously low on fuel and ammunition after three months of sustained combat in the USSR. About 40 per cent of Germany's fuel stocks were consumed during Operation Barbarossa and consumption was fast outstripping production. Ammunition was also in short supply, since Hitler ordered a major reduction in production following the fall of France despite planning for a major campaign against the USSR. By the start of Typhoon, demand for artillery ammunition was exceeding production by a ratio of more than 11:1. During Typhoon, German industry produced 774,000 rounds of large-calibre artillery ammunition but expended over 5 million rounds. By the end of 1941, Germany's stock of artillery ammunition had fallen to its lowest point of the war.

Nor were Army Group Centre's personnel or equipment losses being made good. Although the German Replacement Army was training about 128,000 men per month, the Ostheer was receiving only about one replacement for every two men lost. Guderian's 2nd Panzer Group had suffered 55,380 casualties by 22 November, but it had only received 29,589 replacements. Instead, Hitler was sending many of the replacements to new divisions being formed in occupied Western Europe. German armour production in late 1941 was only slightly ahead of losses but most of the new tanks were also going to new units in the West. Army Group Centre's panzer divisions were only receiving about one replacement tank for every eight lost in combat. In mid-September 1941 OKH authorized the transport of 307 tanks from reserve stocks to replenish Army Group Centre's armour for Typhoon, but these were the only substantial armour replacements received during the battle for Moscow. Thus, even before the onset of winter, Army Group Centre was heading into the decisive battle of the war with under-strength units and worn-out equipment.

The failure of the OKH and OKW to marshal all its available resources and weight the main effort towards Moscow was a major reason for the failure of Typhoon. When Germany needed every soldier for the decisive moment in Russia, some 34 divisions with almost 900,000 troops were left sitting idly in Western Europe guarding against a non-existent British threat. While the Soviet Stavka was able to direct 62 division equivalents to rebuild the shattered Western Front in October–November 1941 the only new units received by Army Group Centre during Typhoon were the Légion des Volontaires Français (LVF) and a few paratroop battalions. Yet the Germans had five idle mountain divisions in Norway and Finland that were well equipped for cold-weather operations.

SOVIET FORCES

The Soviet Army in late September 1941 was a wounded and nearly cornered animal. Virtually the entire pre-war Soviet border armies and their heavy equipment had been obliterated in the first three months of the war. The Soviet Air Force (VVS), while still contesting control of the skies in selected areas, had been shattered in the opening weeks and had yet to regain its full combat effectiveness. Once the enormity of the military catastrophe facing the USSR became apparent, the Stavka headquarters began to frantically recall distant units from all over the far-flung Soviet domain and to mobilize new divisions at an almost unbelievable rate.

Since the start of Barbarossa, the Soviets had lost over 20,000 tanks and 14,000 aircraft. In order to escape the advancing Germans, the bulk of Soviet heavy industry was shipped eastward to the Urals during the late summer of 1941. While the evacuation of Soviet industry preserved Russia's long-term ability to prosecute the war, it had two negative short-term impacts on the defence of Moscow. First, Soviet war production dropped to dangerously low levels during the period September–November 1941 and would not improve until the factories began production in their new locations. Soviet monthly tank production in October–November 1941 was about 160 KV-1/2 heavy tanks, 170 T-34/76 medium tanks, and 320 T-40/60 light tanks. Production of ammunition, artillery and trucks was also severely disrupted. Thus, because of a short-term drop in armaments' production, the Soviets would have to fight the Moscow campaign without their normal material superiority. The second major impact of the industrial evacuation was to divert about 60 per cent of the available railway capacity for three months, leaving little capacity to move in new reinforcement units or to supply front-line units. Until these shortages of armaments and strategic transport were rectified, the Soviets were severely handicapped.

Heavy losses had also required the Soviets to make tactical and structural adjustments to their forces. What little remained of the pre-war tank and mechanized infantry divisions were reorganized as independent tank brigades. Stalin's incessant demands for a counteroffensive to drive out the German invaders obliged Stavka to create a centralized artillery reserve by stripping half of the artillery from front-line rifle divisions. In the long run, the creation of a Stavka-controlled artillery reserve would add great power to Soviet offensives but in the short run, it greatly weakened the defensive firepower of the infantry units defending the approaches to Moscow. Furthermore, the Soviet artillery units had greatly declined in skill because of insufficient training and lack of communication equipment; hastily trained artillery crews could only use direct fire since they lacked training for indirect fire and few radios were available in any case. Indeed, the lack of sufficient radios severely degraded Soviet command and control, and Soviet commanders were often unaware of major German breakthroughs until German tanks approached their headquarters.

Another important Soviet innovation was the creation of the first guards divisions on 18 September 1941. Guards units were an attempt to counter German qualitative superiority by combining the best combat-experienced Soviet troops with the best Soviet weapons and leaders. The Red Air Force also created guards squadrons composed of the most successful pilots and the best aircraft. Initially, guards units had little impact on the Moscow campaign due to their limited number and inadequate equipping, but in time they would play a major role in all Soviet counteroffensives.

The Soviet Army did have some very robust and effective weapons in the T-34/76 tank, the 76.2mm F-22 USV gun, the 122mm howitzer and the BM-13 *Katyusha* multiple rocket launcher. Unfortunately, these fine weapons were not available in quantity during Typhoon and most Soviet troops lacked the training to make good use of the few that were available. Much of the Soviet armour used during Typhoon consisted of only light tanks and a good deal of obsolete artillery was pulled out of storage to replace losses. Rather than armour, the most important Soviet manoeuvre units in Typhoon were the cavalry units, which had more training than most other units and which were not seriously impaired by mud, snow or lack of supplies.

At the start of Typhoon, the Soviet Western, Reserve and Bryansk Fronts had about 864,000 combat troops, 849 tanks (only 94 T-34s and 47 KV-1s) and 364 aircraft – which was almost 50 per cent of the Red Army's front-line strength. The combat power of these three fronts consisted of 95 divisions (83 infantry, two motorized rifle, nine cavalry and one tank) and 14 independent brigades (one motorized rifle and 13 tank). However, the Soviet divisions were even more worn out than the

invading German units and the average infantry division in October 1941 had only about 5,000–6,000 troops. Twelve militia divisions were formed in Moscow and dispatched to the Western Front just prior to the start of Typhoon; these divisions were larger but poorly trained and equipped. The normal Soviet strong suit – artillery – was greatly depleted after three months of war and only 1,997 guns of 107mm calibre or larger were available. Soviet defensive plans were also hindered by the lack of anti-tank and anti-personnel mines, as well as engineer units to construct proper obstacles. Instead, the Soviets relied on civilian labour to construct massive, but poorly designed obstacle belts. Soviet forces around Moscow also suffered from lack of operational mobility due to the shortage of wheeled transport.

Soviet tactical air strength available to support the Western, Bryansk and Reserve Fronts consisted of 201 fighters, 147 bombers, 13 ground-attack and 30 reconnaissance aircraft. Other air assets in the Moscow area consisted of the strategic Long Range Bomber Force (with 154 serviceable bombers) and the 6th PVO Fighter Corps, which had 700 fighters and 870 anti-aircraft guns for the protection of the capital. Inside Moscow, there were 31,000 militia, two NKVD security divisions and a large number of training or cadre units.

While the Soviet Union did possess substantial military forces in the Far East and Caucasus, the limitations placed upon rail capacity by the industrial evacuation programme hindered the ability to transfer substantial forces westward. Furthermore, the impact of the 'Siberians' on Operation Typhoon has been exaggerated. Firstly, the 'Siberians' were neither a large nor battle-experienced cadre of winter-trained troops who arrived at the decisive moment to tip the balance. Rather, most 'Siberian' units were recently raised and lacked significant combat experience or winter training; only the 413th Infantry Division that arrived at the end of October had a large cadre of Nomonhan veterans. Secondly, the 'Siberians' did not appear en masse. Thirdly, very few of the divisions transferred from the Far East went to Moscow; of the seven pre-war divisions sent westward, only two went to Moscow (the 32nd and 78th). The true Soviet 'miracle' in the Moscow campaign was Stavka's ability to generate new – albeit untrained and poorly equipped – combat units.

ABOVE **A Soviet anti-tank team with a PTRD-41 14.5mm anti-tank rifle covers a road bridge from a hasty fighting position. The PTRD-41 was introduced in autumn 1941 and by November Soviet rifle regiments were authorized six each. (From the fonds of the RGAKFD in Krasnogorsk via Nik Cornish)**

ABOVE, LEFT **Soviet rifle troops and armour move up to the front. Note the tank column includes mixed types, including a T-34/76, a BT-7 and a T-26. Soviet armour units in November 1941 were typically composed of whatever tanks were available. (Central Museum of the Armed Forces Moscow via Nik Cornish)**

ORDERS OF BATTLE

German order of battle 2 October 1941

Army Group Centre (Field Marshal von Bock)
Third Panzer Army (Colonel General Reinhardt) [1]
  XLI Panzer Corps (Colonel General Model)
    1st Panzer Division
    36th Motorized Infantry Division
  LVI Motorized Corps (General Schaal)
    6th Panzer Division
    7th Panzer Division
    14th Motorized Infantry Division
    129th Infantry Division
  VI Corps (General Förster)
    6th Infantry Division
    26th Infantry Division
    110th Infantry Division
  V Corps (Colonel General Ruoff)
    5th Infantry Division
    35th Infantry Division
    106th Infantry Division
  Reserve:
    900th Lehr (Mot.) Brigade

Second Panzer Army (Colonel General Guderian)
  XXIV Panzer Corps (General Baron Geyr von Schweppenburg)
    3rd Panzer Division
    4th Panzer Division
    10th Motorized Infantry Division
  XLVII Panzer Corps (General Lemelsen)
    17th Panzer Division
    18th Panzer Division
    29th Motorized Infantry Division
  XLVIII Panzer Corps (General Kempf)
    9th Panzer Division
    16th Motorized Infantry Division
    25th Motorized Infantry Division
  XXXIV Corps (General Metz)
    45th Infantry Division
    134th Infantry Division
  XXXV Corps (Kaempfe)
    1st Cavalry Division
    95th Infantry Division
    262nd Infantry Division
    293rd Infantry Division
    296th Infantry Division

Fourth Panzer Army (Colonel General Hoepner)
  XII Corps (General Schroth)
    34th Infantry Division
    98th Infantry Division
  XL Motorized Corps (General Stumme)
    2nd Panzer Division
    10th Panzer Division
    258th Infantry Division
  XLVI Motorized Corps (General Vietinghoff)
    5th Panzer Division
    11th Panzer Division
    252nd Infantry Division
  LVII Panzer Corps (General Kuntzen)
    SS Reich Motorized Infantry Division
    3rd Motorized Infantry Division
    19th Panzer Division
    20th Panzer Division

Ninth Army (Colonel General Strauss)
  VIII Corps (General Heitz)
    8th Infantry Division
    28th Infantry Division
    87th Infantry Division
  XXIII Corps (General Schubert)
    102nd Infantry Division
    206th Infantry Division
    251st Infantry Division
    256th Infantry Division
  XXVII Corps (General Wäger)
    86th Infantry Division
    162nd Infantry Division
    255th Infantry Division
  Reserve:
    161st Infantry Division

Second Army (Colonel General Baron von Weichs)
  XIII Corps (General Felber)
    17th Infantry Division
    260th Infantry Division
  XLIII Corps (General Heinrici)
    52nd Infantry Division
    131st Infantry Division (-)
  LIII Corps (General Weisenberger)
    31st Infantry Division
    167th Infantry Division
    56th Infantry Division
  Reserve:
    112th Infantry Division

Fourth Army (Field Marshal von Kluge)
  VII Corps (General Fahrmbacher)
    7th Infantry Division
    23rd Infantry Division
    197th Infantry Division
    267th Infantry Division
  IX Corps (General Geyer)
    137th Infantry Division
    183rd Infantry Division
    263rd Infantry Division
    292nd Infantry Division
  XX Corps (General Materna)
    15th Infantry Division
    78th Infantry Division
    268th Infantry Division

Luftflotte 2 (Field Marshal Kesselring):
  II Fliegerkorps (General Loerzer)
    Fighters: II, III/JG 3; I, II, III, IV/JG 51; I JG 52;
    Bombers: I, II/KG3; III KG 26; I KG 28; I, III/KG53; Kampfgruppe 100
    Ground Attack: II/SKG-210; I, II, III/StG77
  VIII Fliegerkorps (General von Richtofen)
    Fighters: II/JG52; II(S)/LG2;
    Bombers: I, 8, 9/KG2; III/KG3
    Ground Attack: II, III/StG1; I, III/StG2

NOTES:
1. Colonel General Hermann Hoth until 5 October.

Soviet order of battle 2 October 1941

Western Front (Lieutenant General Konev)

16th Army (Major General Rokossovsky)
- 38th Rifle Division
- 108th Rifle Division
- 112th Rifle Division
- 214th Rifle Division
- 127th Tank Brigade

19th Army (Lieutenant General Lukin)
- 50th Rifle Division
- 89th Rifle Division
- 91st Rifle Division
- 166th Rifle Division
- 244th Rifle Division

20th Army (Lieutenant General Ershakov)
- 73rd Rifle Division
- 129th Rifle Division
- 144th Rifle Division
- 229th Rifle Division

22nd Army (Major General Iushkevich)
- 126th Rifle Division
- 133rd Rifle Division
- 174th Rifle Division
- 179th Rifle Division
- 186th Rifle Division
- 256th Rifle Division

29th Army (Lieutenant General Maslennikov)
- 178th Rifle Division
- 243rd Rifle Division
- 246th Rifle Division
- 252nd Rifle Division

30th Army (Major General Khomenko)
- 162nd Rifle Division
- 242nd Rifle Division
- 250th Rifle Division
- 251st Rifle Division

Dovator's Cavalry Group (Major General Dovator)
- 45th Cavalry Division
- 50th Cavalry Division
- 53rd Cavalry Division
- 101st Mechanized Division
- 107th Mechanized Division
- 126th Tank Brigade
- 128th Tank Brigade
- 143rd Tank Brigade

Western Front Reserves:
- 5th Guards Rifle Division
- 134th Rifle Division
- 152nd Rifle Division

Reserve Front (Marshal Budenny)

24th Army (Major General Rakutin)
- 19th Rifle Division
- 103rd Rifle Division
- 106th Rifle Division
- 139th Rifle Division
- 160th Rifle Division (second formation)
- 170th Rifle Division
- 309th Rifle Division
- 144th Tank Brigade
- 146th Tank Brigade
- 138th Tank Battalion
- 139th Tank Battalion

31st Army (Major General Dalmatov)
- 5th Rifle Division
- 110th Rifle Division
- 119th Rifle Division
- 247th Rifle Division
- 249th Rifle Division

32nd Army (Major General Vishnevskiy)
- 2nd Rifle Division
- 8th Rifle Division
- 29th Rifle Division
- 140th Rifle Division

33rd Army (Major General Onuprienko)
- 17th Rifle Division
- 18th Rifle Division
- 60th Rifle Division
- 113th Rifle Division
- 173rd Rifle Division

43rd Army (Lieutenant General Sobennikov)
- 53rd Rifle Division
- 149th Rifle Division
- 211th Rifle Division
- 222nd Rifle Division
- 145th Tank Brigade
- 148 Tank Brigade

49th Army (Lieutenant General Zakharkin)
- 194th Rifle Division
- 220th Rifle Division
- 248th Rifle Division
- 303rd Rifle Division
- 29th Cavalry Division
- 31st Cavalry Division

Front Reserves
- 147th Tank Brigade

Bryansk Front (Lieutenant General Yeremenko)

3rd Army (Major General Kreizer)
- 137th Rifle Division
- 148th Rifle Division
- 269th Rifle Division
- 280th Rifle Division
- 282nd Rifle Division
- 4th Cavalry Division
- 855th Rifle Regiment/278th Rifle Division

13th Army (Major General Gorodniansky)
- 6th Rifle Division
- 121st Rifle Division
- 132nd Rifle Division
- 143rd Rifle Division
- 155th Rifle Division
- 298th Rifle Division
- 307th Rifle Division
- 55th Cavalry Division
- 141st Tank Brigade

50th Army (Major General Petrov)
- 217th Rifle Division
- 258th Rifle Division
- 260th Rifle Division
- 278th Rifle Division (-)
- 279th Rifle Division
- 290th Rifle Division
- 299th Rifle Division
- 108th Tank Division

Operational Group Ermakov (Major General A. Ermakov)
- 2nd Guards Rifle Division
- 160th Rifle Division (first formation)
- 283rd Rifle Division
- 21st Mountain Cavalry Division
- 52nd Cavalry Division
- 121st Tank Brigade
- 150th Tank Brigade

Front Reserves:
- 7th Guards Rifle Division
- 154th Rifle Division
- 287th Rifle Division
- 42nd Tank Brigade

VVS supporting Moscow fronts:
- 18 x fighter regiments
- 12 x bomber regiments
- 7 x ground-attack regiments

THE SURPRISE OFFENSIVE
30 SEPTEMBER – 15 OCTOBER 1941

GUDERIAN ROUTS OPERATIONAL GROUP ERMAKOV

Despite the heavy use of Guderian's 2nd Panzer Group in the Kiev encirclement, von Bock decided to use this highly experienced but tired formation for the main effort of the drive on Moscow. Guderian had to hustle to get his exhausted and dispersed forces into their jumping-off positions on time and he was not entirely successful. A Soviet spoiling attack required Guderian to commit XLVIII Panzer Corps to screen his right flank around Putivl and consequently, he would begin his offensive with only XXIV and XLVII Panzer Corps. Guderian's left flank was virtually in the air, with the 1st Cavalry Division screening a 60km-wide sector between his Panzer Group and von Weichs' Second Army.

Guderian's 2nd Panzer Group represented the cream of the Wehrmacht and included five panzer and four motorized infantry divisions and the Grossdeutschland motorized infantry regiment. Six infantry divisions in XXXIV and XXXV Corps would also arrive soon to protect Guderian's flanks. Despite extensive combat and mechanical losses in the Kiev fighting, Guderian still had over 300 tanks available at the start of the offensive, giving him a 10:1 local superiority in armour. Indeed, the Soviets were less of an immediate concern than fuel and Guderian was forced to begin the offensive with negligible reserves of fuel. Guderian's main railhead was Konotop, some 80km to the rear. He intended to attack with XXIV Panzer Corps as his main effort, driving

A German infantry squad clears out a burning Russian village in the early days of Operation Typhoon. The *Unteroffizier* squad leader is in front armed with an MP40 machine pistol. (Nik Cornish at Stavka)

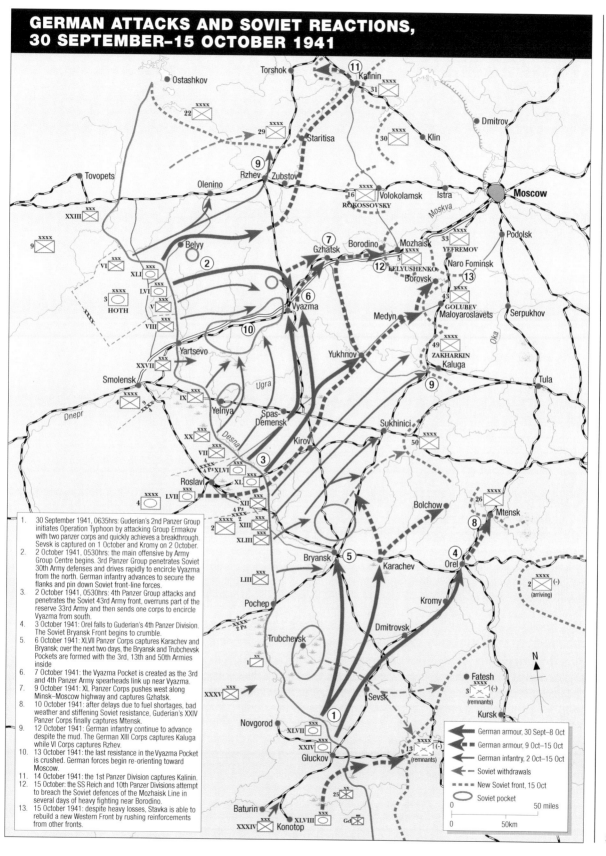

GERMAN ATTACKS AND SOVIET REACTIONS, 30 SEPTEMBER–15 OCTOBER 1941

1. 30 September 1941, 0635hrs: Guderian's 2nd Panzer Group initiates Operation Typhoon by attacking Group Ermakov with two panzer corps and quickly achieves a breakthrough. Sevsk is captured on 1 October and Kromy on 2 October.
2. 2 October 1941, 0530hrs: the main offensive by Army Group Centre begins. 3rd Panzer Group penetrates Soviet 30th Army defenses and drives rapidly to encircle Vyazma from the north. German infantry advances to secure the flanks and pin down Soviet front-line forces.
3. 2 October 1941, 0530hrs: 4th Panzer Group attacks and penetrates the Soviet 43rd Army front, overruns part of the reserve 33rd Army and then sends one corps to encircle Vyazma from south.
4. 3 October 1941: Orel falls to Guderian's 4th Panzer Division. The Soviet Bryansk Front begins to crumble.
5. 6 October 1941: XLVII Panzer Corps captures Karachev and Bryansk; over the next two days, the Bryansk and Trubchevsk Pockets are formed with the 3rd, 13th and 50th Armies inside
6. 7 October 1941: the Vyazma Pocket is created as the 3rd and 4th Panzer Army spearheads link up near Vyazma.
7. 9 October 1941: XL Panzer Corps pushes west along Minsk–Moscow highway and captures Gzhatsk.
8. 10 October 1941: after delays due to fuel shortages, bad weather and stiffening Soviet resistance, Guderian's XXIV Panzer Corps finally captures Mtensk.
9. 12 October 1941: German infantry continue to advance despite the mud. The German XIII Corps captures Kaluga while VI Corps captures Rzhev.
10. 13 October 1941: the last resistance in the Vyazma Pocket is crushed. German forces begin re-orienting toward Moscow.
11. 14 October 1941: the 1st Panzer Division captures Kalinin.
12. 15 October: the SS Reich and 10th Panzer Divisions attempt to breach the Soviet defences of the Mozhaisk Line in several days of heavy fighting near Borodino.
13. 15 October 1941: despite heavy losses, Stavka is able to rebuild a new Western Front by rushing reinforcements from other fronts.

German armour, 30 Sept–8 Oct
German armour, 9 Oct–15 Oct
German infantry, 2 Oct–15 Oct
Soviet withdrawals
New Soviet front, 15 Oct
Soviet pocket

0   50 miles
0   50km

N

German PzKpfw II and PzKpfw III tanks in an assembly area during the early phase of Operation Typhoon. These PzKpfw IIIF tanks are still armed with the 37mm gun, rather than the better 50mm gun. (Nik Cornish at Stavka)

from Glukhov, penetrating the left flank of the Bryansk Front and then exploiting towards Orel. XLVII Panzer Corps would launch a supporting attack to the left of XXIV Panzer Corps, tearing through the left flank of the Soviet 13th Army near Jampol, then swinging north-west to take Bryansk from the rear. XLVIII Panzer Corps would screen Guderian's eastern flank during the drive on Orel. Although German intelligence was unsure about the state of Soviet reserves behind the front, Guderian was aware of the dispositions of all Soviet forces to his immediate front.

The Soviet High Command had not expected Guderian to pivot north again after the Kiev fighting – their attention was now focused on the Ukraine – and Group Ermakov had been ordered to launch spoiling attacks against Guderian's extended flank. The five divisions in Major General Arkadii Ermakov's operational group (three infantry, two cavalry and two tank brigades) had not dug in their troops or artillery. Soviet tactical intelligence at this point was very poor and they missed the redeployment and reorientation of Guderian's armour.

Guderian began his offensive at 0635hrs on 30 September, with his two panzer corps striking the unsuspecting Soviets. Two 210mm howitzer battalions provided an artillery preparation and Luftwaffe close air support hit the Soviet lines of communication hard. The main *Schwerpunkt*, Kampfgruppe Eberbach of 4th Panzer Division, attacked the newly raised 283rd Rifle Division and inexperienced 150th Tank Brigade in the flat terrain near Essman.[2] On the flanks of the *Schwerpunkt*, 3rd Panzer Division dispersed the 121st Tank Brigade and the 10th Motorized Infantry Division attempted to pin down the two cavalry divisions of Group Ermakov. Due to poor communications and limited reconnaissance capabilities, Ermakov thought his group was being attacked by only a single German corps and sent this faulty information to the front commander, Lieutenant General Yeremenko. Based upon Ermakov's inaccurate reporting, Yeremenko assessed Guderian's attack to be a diversion and decided not to commit any substantial reserves to this area. Instead, Ermakov was ordered to launch a local counterattack to repulse the German penetration but a puny and uncoordinated counterattack by 30 light tanks near Sevsk on 1 October only resulted in the destruction of Ermakov's remaining armour. One panzer company even managed to overrun a regiment of 122mm howitzers, which was caught in the open. Eberbach's panzers seized Sevsk

An abandoned Soviet T-26S light tank, which was an improved model introduced in 1938 and featured a new conical turret, sloped armour and a radio. Each pre-war Soviet rifle division had one company of these tanks. (Nik Cornish)

at noon on 1 October, completing the breakthrough of the Soviet Bryansk Front's left flank. Without a prepared defence, Ermakov's divisions fell back in disorder towards Orel and Bryansk, thereby uncovering the flank of the Soviet 13th Army on their right flank.

Baron Geyr von Schweppenburg's XXIV Panzer Corps continued the attack, with the transportation hub of Orel as its first operational objective. With little remaining opposition in its path, the 34th Motorcycle Infantry Battalion raced 100km up the Orel highway, to seize the large bridge over the Oka River at Kromy at dusk on 2 October. The next morning, Kampfgruppe Eberbach pushed on to Orel, a city of 110,000. Orel had virtually no defences and the people were stunned to see German tanks driving into the city. By 1600hrs on 3 October, the 6th Company, 35th Panzer Regiment, had occupied the city centre. In four days, 4th Panzer Division had moved 240km and inflicted 2,200 casualties on the enemy, while capturing 16 tanks and 24 artillery pieces for the loss of only 41 killed and 120 wounded.

On Guderian's left flank, Lemelsen's XLVII Panzer Corps struck the 298th Rifle Division with both the 17th and 18th Panzer Divisions. The 298th Rifle Division was typical of many Soviet divisions in October 1941 – incompletely equipped and partly trained. The division was quickly overrun and the 13th Army's line was penetrated. Major General Avksentii Gorodniansky, the commander of the 13th Army, committed the 141st Tank Brigade to counterattack but the unit's handful of light tanks were quickly knocked out. With Group Ermakov retiring on his left flank and his own centre giving way, Gorodniansky ordered 13th Army to retire northward towards Bryansk. With the Soviets in retreat, XLVII Panzer Corps rapidly rolled up the 13th Army and pushed hard for Karachev to cut the Orel–Bryansk highway. By 3 October, Guderian's spearheads had completely unhinged the left flank of the Soviet Bryansk Front. In the first five days of the offensive, Second Panzer Army captured 9,300 Soviet troops, 60 tanks and 109 artillery pieces.

FOURTH PANZER ARMY'S ATTACK

The remainder of Army Group Centre began Operation Typhoon at 0530hrs on 2 October, with simultaneous attacks by two panzer armies and three infantry armies on a 600km-wide front; it was one of the largest German offensives in the entire war. The main ground attacks were preceded by an artillery preparation and Luftwaffe air strikes on forward Soviet troop concentrations.

Hoepner's Fourth Panzer Army was assigned the mission of breaking through the defences of the 43rd Army of Marshal Budenny's Reserve Front, defeating Soviet second-echelon forces and then forming the right pincer round the south side of Vyazma. Stumme's XL Panzer Corps (2nd and 10th Panzer Divisions) was the Fourth Panzer Army's main effort. General Heinrich von Vietinghoff's XLVI Panzer Corps, with about 230 tanks in the 5th and 11th Panzer Divisions, was to advance on the left flank of XL Panzer Corps. XII Corps, with two infantry divisions, was to protect the right flank of XL Panzer Corps. In reserve around Roslavl, General Adolf Kuntzen's LVII Panzer Corps was ready to exploit the breakthrough. The main supply railhead near Roslavl was about 25km behind Fourth Panzer Army's assembly areas, which greatly enhanced the formation's initial logistic situation.

Lieutenant General Petr Sobennikov's 43rd Army occupied a very wide 85km front with only four rifle divisions and two tank brigades. The Soviet troops on the Reserve Front had over a month to dig in behind the Desna River and the heavily forested terrain in the area favoured the defence. Normally, crossing a river under fire and penetrating a fortified zone is a very difficult operation, but Fourth Panzer Army was able to break the 43rd Army's defences in little more than a day. XL Panzer Corps crossed the Desna and struck the Soviet 53rd and 149th Rifle Divisions. Although these were two relatively steady pre-war divisions, both were quickly overrun by a mass of over 560 German tanks on a

A PzKpfw II escorting a supply column through a wooded area. Thousands of Soviet soldiers were cut off behind German lines as a result of the Vyazma–Bryansk encirclements and the German rear areas were far from secure. (Nik Cornish at Stavka)

narrow 25km-wide attack front. The presence of the 2nd and 5th Panzer Divisions, both at full strength and rested after rebuilding in France, added great power to Fourth Panzer Army's attack. In vain, Sobennikov ordered his only mobile reserves – the 145th and 148th Tank Brigades – to counterattack the penetration, but they were quickly reduced to combat ineffectiveness. The Soviet tendency to throw armour piecemeal into hasty counterattacks during the initial stages of Typhoon only played into German hands, since it exposed small numbers of tanks to be destroyed piecemeal by the Luftwaffe and German anti-tank gunners; much of the Soviet armour reserves were just thrown away in amateurish counterattacks. Once the 43rd Army's armour was spent, Fourth Panzer Army advanced rapidly towards its first operational objective – the rail junction at Spas-Demensk. Meanwhile, the German XII Corps infantry mopped up the disorganized remnants of the 43rd Army.

The rapidity with which the Soviet Reserve Front collapsed only served to confirm the OKH's intelligence estimates that predicted an imminent collapse. Major General Onuprienko's 33rd Army, with five rifle divisions, was a second-echelon formation deployed between Spas-Demensk and Kirov that should have been able to prevent any exploitation of the breakthrough in the 43rd Army's sector. However, the Soviet reserve divisions were deployed like beads on a string in a dispersed arc and were not dug in. Three of the five rifle divisions were recently raised militia units. Stumme's XL Panzer Corps simply overran one division at a time beginning on 3 October and within two days the 33rd Army had been roughly shoved out of the path of Fourth Panzer Army's *Schwerpunkt*. XLVI Panzer Corps and XII Corps further widened the breach in the Reserve Front's sector and by 5 October Hoepner was ready to commit his exploitation force, LVII Panzer Corps.

THIRD PANZER ARMY'S ATTACK

Third Panzer Army also began its participation in Typhoon with an artillery preparation at 0530hrs on 2 October. Colonel General Hermann Hoth commanded Third Panzer Army for the first three days of the offensive, until he went to Army Group South to command Seventeenth Army and was replaced by Colonel General Reinhardt. Hoth's army had only two panzer corps available and he would initially leave his motorized infantry divisions in reserve. Hoth's mission was to break through the Western Front's 19th and 30th Armies, defeat the second-echelon forces and then pivot and sweep behind Vyazma to link up with Fourth Panzer Army. At the start of Typhoon, Hoth's main supply railhead was near Smolensk, about 50km to the south.

Hoth's main effort was General Ferdinand Schaal's LVI Panzer Corps, with the 6th and 7th Panzer Divisions up front and the 14th Motorized Infantry Division in reserve. Schaal had about 250 panzers operational, mostly Czech-built PzKpfw 35(t) and PzKpfw 38(t) models, yet when the corps attacked the Soviet 91st Rifle Division of Lieutenant General Lukin's 19th Army it was able to advance about 5–10km on the first day. On Schaal's left flank, Colonel General Model's XLI Panzer Corps attacked the Soviet 162nd Rifle Division with the 1st Panzer Division and the 129th Infantry Division. Although Schaal's and Model's attacks were

much weaker than the other German armoured spearheads, and against a numerically superior and dug-in enemy, the Germans split the seam between the 19th and 30th Soviet Armies and were able to rip it wide open in less than two days. Hoth's offensive relied much more on infantry attacks than the other two panzer groups – partly due to the weakness of his armour and partly due to the forest and lake terrain. On Hoth's left, General Otto Förster's VI Corps attacked the front of Major General Vasilii Khomenko's 30th Army and pinned the front-line divisions down while 1st Panzer penetrated the main line of resistance. On Hoth's right, Ruoff's V Corps attacked with three infantry divisions and was able to push the 19th Army's front-line divisions back, thereby widening the gap for LVI Panzer Corps. Once the Western Front's main defensive belt was pierced, the first operational objective of Third Panzer Army was the bridges over the Dnepr River at Kholm-Zhirkovski. By late on 3 October, LVI Panzer Corps had captured the bridges intact and was well positioned to advance towards the main objective – the encirclement of Vyazma. The rest of Hoth's army continued to eliminate the remnants of the 19th and 30th Armies' infantry in their sector while dealing with local counterattacks.

GERMAN INFANTRY ARMY ATTACKS

The three German infantry armies also had their roles to play in the opening days of Typhoon, although less dramatically than the panzer groups. Von Bock preferred to avoid heavy casualties from frontal attacks on fortified Soviet lines, so he ordered that most of the infantry would be held back until the panzers had thoroughly disrupted the Western Front. Once the Soviet armies began to retreat, the three infantry armies would spring forward and crush them in the ensuing pocket battles.

Colonel General Strauss' Ninth Army was deployed with two corps on the right flank of Third Panzer Army and one corps on its left. Strauss' army did not attack until 4 October and its role was strictly limited to

A captured Soviet GAZ-AAA truck in German service on a muddy road in autumn 1941. The Germans had captured thousands of Soviet trucks and they performed better than most German trucks under these primitive conditions. (Nik Cornish)

pinning as many of the Western Front's front-line divisions as possible in order to shape the coming encirclement battle. While the three infantry divisions of General Wäger's XXVII Corps conducted a demonstration against the heavily fortified 16th Army positions around Yartsevo, General Heitz's VIII Corps conducted a two-division infiltration attack in the boundary between the Soviet 16th and 19th Armies. Only two of the Ninth Army's divisions were heavily engaged but the effort seems to have succeeded in fixing the bulk of the Soviet 16th Army in place.

Colonel General Baron von Weichs' Second Army began a series of fixing attacks against Major General Mikhail Petrov's 50th Army in order to prevent the Bryansk Front from shifting troops to deal with Guderian's panzer breakthrough to the south-west. The Second Army attacked with five of its eight infantry divisions on 3 October, with Weisenberger's LIII Corps the main effort, pushing directly eastward to Bryansk. The Soviets had long expected a direct thrust on Bryansk down the main road from Roslavl and the defences here were very strong. By 5 October, von Weichs' infantry had advanced little but had forced Yeremenko to commit his best reserve, the 108th Tank Division, to stop LIII Corps' advance. With Lemelsen's panzers already approaching the south-east suburbs of Bryansk, von Weichs had achieved his objective of keeping the Bryansk Front focused on him instead of Guderian.

Field Marshal von Kluge's Fourth Army did not attack until 4/5 October, when he committed eight of his ten infantry divisions against the Soviet 20th and 24th Armies in the Yelnya area. On paper, von Kluge was attacking more than a dozen entrenched divisions with only eight divisions – normally a recipe for defeat. However, von Kluge was an expert at preparing set-piece infantry and artillery attacks and his army was better rested and supplied than the other armies in Army Group Center. While Geyer's IX Corps attacked on the left to pin the Soviet 20th Army in Yelnya, XX and VII Corps penetrated the 24th and 43rd Armies' sectors and started rolling up the flank of the 20th Army. Materna's XX Corps was the main effort and it was able to penetrate Major General Rakutin's 24th Army and encircle Soviet forces in Yelnya.

Without any substantial armour support, von Kluge was able to crush and destroy four rifle divisions and the T-34-equipped 145th Tank Brigade by 5 October. Von Kluge's attack was a major success in crumpling the left flank of the Western Front and in setting the stage for the encirclement of Vyazma. Fourth Army suffered 198 officer casualties in just two days of attacking, including IX Corps commander General Geyer and 183rd Infantry Division commander Major General Dippold.

THE SOVIET REACTION

At first, the reaction of Stalin and the Stavka to the start of Typhoon was muted, since most of their attention was still focused on the critical situations at Leningrad and in the Ukraine. Indeed, so unconcerned – or unaware – was Stalin with the significance of Guderian's breakthrough, that on 1 October he ordered the Reserve Front to transfer the entire 49th Army to defend Kursk and Kharkov. It was only when the German attacks started occurring on 2 October along the entire Western, Reserve and Bryansk Fronts that the Stavka grew concerned. They ordered Major General Dmitri Lelyushenko, an experienced armour officer, to head to Orel and take command of several RVGK (Reserve of the Supreme High Command) reserve units hastily forming there as the 1st Guards Rifle Corps.

In the south, Yeremenko was not fully aware of the extent of Guderian's breakthrough, since very few Soviet units were in contact with Second Panzer Army after 1 October. However, Soviet air reconnaissance did detect German panzer columns heading north towards Bryansk and Orel, so Yeremenko started shifting some of his limited reserves. Two rifle divisions from the 13th Army were ordered to move east to block the XLVII Panzer Corps' advance through Seredina Buda, but by the time the sluggish Soviet infantry started moving, the panzers had already bypassed them. Yeremenko also tried to move another rifle division and some armour remnants to block the main highway into Bryansk from the south,

Soviet infantry establishing a Maxim machine-gun position west of Moscow in October 1941. Numerous small blocking detachments like this one were sacrificed in order to buy time for the Red Army to recover. (Central Museum of the Armed Forces Moscow via Nik Cornish)

Soviet infantry moving into a battle position. Each Soviet infantry battalion was authorized 12 heavy water-cooled M1910 Maxim-Sokolov 7.62mm machine guns. The weapon was heavy and clumsy compared to the German MG34. (From the fonds of the RGAKFD in Krasnogorsk via Nik Cornish)

but he was unaware that the closest German panzers were actually approaching the city from the east.

In the north, Konev scrambled to throw everything he had against Hoth's Third Panzer Army as soon as he realized that the Germans had achieved a major breakthrough. Konev ordered Lieutenant General Mikhail Lukin, commander of the 19th Army in Hoth's path, to use his three RVGK howitzer regiments (about 100 152mm howitzers) to fire against the German spearheads. Unfortunately for the Western Front, the Soviet artillery had lost much of its ability to conduct indirect fire at this point, particularly against a moving target. When artillery failed to stop Hoth's panzers, Konev turned to his manoeuvre forces to cut off the German spearheads. Konev had over 400 tanks at his disposal, but most were light T-26s. Konev's best tank unit, the 143rd Tank Brigade with about 30 T-34s, was mistakenly sent against the German VIII Corps, instead of the panzer spearhead. Konev then ordered his deputy, Lieutenant General Ivan Boldin, to organize a counterattack force from Western Front reserves and Major General L. Dovator's cavalry group. Major General Khomenko's 30th Army was also ordered to coordinate a two-division counterattack with Boldin's operational group.

On 4/5 October, Boldin's operational group (which comprised two rifle divisions, a depleted motorized division and two light tank battalions) attacked Schaal's LVI Panzer Corps' bridgehead over the Dnepr near Kholm-Zhirkovski from the south-east while Khomenko attacked from the north-east with two rifle divisions and some cavalry. Despite desperate Soviet attacks, Boldin's group not only failed to repulse the 6th and 7th Panzer Divisions, but also lost 80 tanks. LVI Panzer Corps followed up the Soviet repulse by overrunning much of the Soviet artillery. After less than four days' fighting, Konev's Western Front was split open and he could not close the gap. Chaos reigned in Soviet forward headquarters, particularly due to the lack of sufficient radios and trained staff officers. The bulk of the Soviet infantry in the Western Front simply remained in their positions until they were either overrun or surrounded.

The situation was even worse in the centre of the front, where Marshal Budenny's front-line armies were quickly rolled up, while his second-

echelon forces threw away their few mobile troops in futile counterattacks. As the left-flank armies of the Western Front starting pulling back towards Vyazma, the Reserve Front armies sat immobile. Fourth Panzer Army seized Kirov and Spas-Demensk on 4 October and then leapt forward to capture an intact bridge over the Ugra River at Yukhnov. A large part of the problem was that most of Budenny's units were either remnants of divisions reduced in the Smolensk battles or militia units that were still in the process of forming; very few of the Reserve Front's second-echelon divisions were actually capable of serious combat operations at the start of Typhoon. Furthermore, the Reserve Front had been stripped of fuel, ammunition and transport in favour of other commands.

By 4 October, it was clear that the Soviet Western and Bryansk Fronts were in real trouble but Stalin refused to order any withdrawals. As it became more obvious on 5 October that a catastrophe was approaching, Stalin finally allowed the Stavka to order a withdrawal towards Vyazma to save the Western Front. However, Stalin was disgusted with the miserable performance of Konev's command and he recalled General Zhukov from Leningrad to replace him. Indeed, Stalin considered executing Konev, as he had Pavlov for the Bialystok–Minsk encirclements in June.

The only place that the Stavka was able to slow the initial German attack was near the town of Mtensk, north-east of Orel. On the morning of 3 October, the Stavka ordered the 5th Airborne Corps to move its 10th and 201st Brigades by air to the Orel airfield and link up with Lelyushenko's 1st Guard Rifle Corps, which was moving in by rail. The Soviets used 80 TB-3 bombers to move about 5,000 paratroopers by air in several lifts – a truly amazing achievement by the standards of 1941. However, as the 201st Airborne Brigade started landing at Orel airfield around 1600hrs on 3 October, it came under fire from the lead elements of Kampfgruppe Eberbach. Only a few hundred paratroopers were landed at Orel's airfield and the rest diverted to a secondary field north of the city. Once on the ground, Colonel Stepan Gurev's paratroopers linked up with the 132nd NKVD Border Guard Regiment and established a blocking position north of the city, on the Orel–Tula highway. The Soviet paratroopers and NKVD troops were trained soldiers but they had only a few 45mm anti-tank guns and 82mm mortars to halt Guderian's armoured spearhead.

At the start of Typhoon, the Reserve of the Supreme High Command (RVGK) was virtually depleted, since three new armies had just been formed on the Volkhov Front near Leningrad and many other divisions were sent to the Ukraine to rebuild the shattered Southern Front. At the start of October 1941, Stalin and the Stavka felt that Moscow was well protected and kept few regular units actually near the capital. However once the front fell apart in a matter of days, the Stavka had to scramble to find stable reinforcements that would not merely join the stampede to the rear. The only decent units in the vicinity of the capital were the newly designated 5th and 6th Guards Rifle Divisions and the new 11th Tank Brigade with T-34/76 tanks; these units received movement orders for Orel on 1 October but did not begin arriving until 5/6 October. Oddly, it was Colonel Katukov's 4th Tank Brigade, moving by rail from Stalingrad that was the first heavy reinforcement to reach the Orel area. Katukov's brigade offloaded at the Mtensk rail station on 4 October and he quickly sent two small armoured battle groups down the highway to support the paratroopers' roadblock. Lelyushenko remained in Mtensk, coordinating the arrival of the rest of his corps and establishing a new defensive line on the Zusha River. On the morning of 5 October, Kampfgruppe Eberbach started probing up the highway and after several hours' skirmishing, the mixed Soviet force withdrew back to Naryshkino, where Katukov had been assembling the rest of his brigade and a battalion of the 11th Tank Brigade. For the first time during Typhoon, the Soviets had been able to mass more than 40 T-34/76 and KV-1 tanks in one place and Katukov anticipated giving Kampfgruppe Eberbach quite a surprise the next morning.

THE VYAZMA–BRYANSK POCKETS ARE FORMED

6 October 1941 was a day of disaster for the Soviet Western, Bryansk and Reserve Fronts. Konev issued orders for the 16th, 19th and 20th Armies to begin pulling back towards Vyazma but most of the units were fixed in place by German infantry attacks from the Fourth and Ninth Armies and had difficulty disengaging. The Soviet 32nd Army from Budenny's Reserve Front had four rifle divisions deployed in an arc around Vyazma that should have been able to hold the routes into the city as the front-line units withdrew to the east. However, the 32nd Army's divisions were all militia units that had just begun converting into regular units and they completely collapsed in the face of unexpected armour attacks from the north and south. By 2000hrs on 6 October, Colonel Hasso von Manteuffel's motorized infantry *Kampfgruppe* from the 7th Panzer Division had cut the Minsk highway just north of Vyazma. Meanwhile, XL and XLI Panzer Corps seized the road junction at Spas-Demensk and pushed rapidly to the north-east. On 5 October, a Soviet Pe 2 light bomber spotted a column of hundreds of German vehicles moving

A German infantry column passing Soviet prisoners marching westward in the autumn of 1941. Army Group Centre claimed to have captured 673,098 Soviet troops in the Vyazma–Bryansk Pockets and initially the offensive appeared to be a major success. (Nik Cornish at Stavka)

unopposed up the Moscow–Warsaw highway – and reported no Soviet units anywhere in sight. The reports were discounted as false – which indicates how poor Soviet tactical reporting was at this critical point – until the 10th Panzer Division captured the city of Yukhnov and its bridges over the Ugra River at 0530hrs on 6 October. In Moscow, Stalin was shocked to realize that German tanks were less than 200km from his capital.

At 1030hrs on 7 October, 10th Panzer Division advanced into Vyazma against weak resistance from Soviet rear-echelon troops and linked up with 7th Panzer Division, thereby forming the Vyazma Pocket. The bulk of the 16th, 19th, 20th and 32nd Soviet Armies were caught in this pocket, as well as remnants of the 24th Army. Inside the Vyazma Pocket, or in several smaller pockets nearby, were some 30 divisions, but they had little leadership. Konev and most of his Western Front staff were evacuated from Vyazma just before the trap closed and Boldin was ordered to organize a breakout to the east. Although Boldin was able to organize several regimental-sized attacks, he could not mount a coordinated breakout effort. By the evening of 7 October, five Germany infantry corps (V, VII, VIII, IX and XXVII Corps) had moved up to begin the *Kessel* (cauldron or pocket) battle.

Zhukov arrived in Moscow at dusk on 7 October and met with Stalin. The mood in the Kremlin was grim. Stalin said that, 'just like Pavlov at the beginning of the war, Konev has opened up the front to the enemy'. Zhukov was shocked to hear Stalin raise the issue of a separate peace with Germany if the situation got much worse. Shaposhnikov directed Zhukov to go to the front and assess what was left of the Western and Reserve Fronts. Shaposhnikov also ordered the transfer of 14 rifle divisions and 16 tank brigades from the RVGK reserve or other fronts, although this would take weeks to implement. Zhukov reached the new Western Front headquarters near Mozhaisk early on 8 October and reported back to Shaposhnikov that the road to Moscow was virtually unprotected and that the defences of the Mozhaisk Line were too weak to stop a determined attack.

The situation was equally grim in the south, where on the morning of 6 October, the 17th Panzer Division advanced unexpectedly into

The 88mm Flak 36 dual-purpose gun was the one German weapon that could defeat the T-34/76 or KV-1 tanks, but the 4th Panzer Division lost two 88mm guns near Mtensk on 6 October 1941 to Katukov's T-34s. (Author's collection)

Bryansk from the east and captured the city of 87,000 in a *coup de main*. Indeed, the attack was so sudden that Yeremenko was not aware of German forces in the vicinity until his headquarters was overrun by panzers and he was wounded. Yeremenko was able to make his way on foot to the 3rd Army positions to the south, but the Bryansk Front lost its leadership at a critical moment. With Bryansk captured and XLVII Panzer Corps behind the Soviet 3rd, 13th and 50th Armies, von Bock ordered von Weichs to attack the front of these Soviet armies and form a pocket around Bryansk. However, the Germans had considerably fewer forces in the southern part of the front than the northern part, and von Weichs' infantry had difficulty pinning the Soviet units in place. In the end, two loose pockets starting forming on 8 October, with the bulk of the 50th Army encircled just north of Bryansk by Heinrici's XLIII Corps and the 18th Panzer Division, and the 3rd and 13th Armies cut off around Trubchevsk by Weisenberger's LIII Corps and the rest of XLVII Panzer Corps. However, Guderian put little effort into fully enclosing the two pockets – he had made the same mistake at Smolensk in July – and far more Soviet troops would escape from the Bryansk–Trubchevsk Pockets than the Vyazma Pocket. Guderian would later come to regret – but not admit – this mistake.

GUDERIAN LOSES THE INITIATIVE

While the bulk of Army Group Centre was involved in the *Kessel* battles of 6–12 October, Guderian still had his XXIV and XLVIII Panzer Corps available. However, Second Panzer Army's supply situation was catastrophic, since the forward units had run out of fuel and were very low on ammunition by 3 October – four days before the first mud or snow. Guderian had started Typhoon with minimal reserves of fuel and ammunition and these had been expended in the drive to Orel. Furthermore, in order to sustain the Second Panzer Army's spearhead – XXIV Panzer Corps – Guderian had to deprive the other corps of their fair share of the available fuel; consequently, XLVIII Panzer Corps was unable to participate in any meaningful way in the first three weeks of Typhoon.

It is worth examining the supply status of the 4th Panzer Division in some detail because it gives insight into the real reasons for Typhoon's ultimate failure. Just prior to the start of Typhoon, the 4th Panzer Division received 162m³ of fuel (1m³ equals 1,000 litres of fuel) and it had an 80m³ reserve carried in its three organic fuel transport companies. The basic load of fuel or *Verbrauchssatz* (abbreviated 1 V.S.) that would enable every vehicle in a panzer division to move 100km was 125m³. German doctrine stated that a panzer unit should have 4 V.S. on hand for offensive operations, but the 4th Panzer Division started Typhoon with 242m³ on hand – slightly less than 2 V.S. The initial attack and advance to Orel, a distance of about 200km, consumed the 2 V.S of fuel available, leaving the division completely immobilized. Now, the nearest source of fuel resupply was in Novgorod-Seversky, a distance of 230km one way. The 4th Panzer Division promptly dispatched its now empty fuel trucks back to the supply base; its supply columns had about 30 trucks that could carry 75m³ of fuel. Convoying to Novgorod-Seversky and back to Orel required at least 15 hours, and the trucks would

In 1941, each Soviet rifle regiment had an anti-tank battery with six 45mm M1937 anti-tank guns. Here, the crew is loading UO-243 HE-FRAG rounds but the primary ammunition was the UB-242/243 series APHE-T round. (Central Museum of the Armed Forces Moscow via Nik Cornish)

consume part of the fuel on the way back. Since the division could only transport about 0.5 V.S. with its own transport, it would normally take at least two days to restock one basic load of fuel and ammunition. On 5 October, Guderian asked the Luftwaffe to fly 500m³ of fuel to Orel to resupply the 4th Panzer Division but Soviet fighter attacks were too frequent on the airfield to risk landing fuel-laden Ju 52 transports. Thus, the farther German armies tried to operate from their railheads, the worse their supply shortfalls became and it was also not unusual for the supply columns to reach the railhead and find that no supply trains had arrived from Germany that day. Thus, Guderian's spearhead spent two critical, good-weather days sitting in Orel because it had no fuel. The standard German lament 'we were stopped by the mud' is nonsense, because Army Group Centre's main effort was stopped dead on its tracks four days before a snowflake fell.

By the evening of 5 October, the 4th Panzer Division's supply columns had been able to make one trip and back to Novgorod-Seversky, restoring minimal mobility to Kampfgruppe Eberbach. However, the 4th Panzer Division took most of 3rd Panzer Division's fuel allotment as well, leaving that division stranded outside Orel for several days. Eberbach's reconnaissance elements became active on the morning of 5 October and they caused the Soviet blocking force to withdraw to Naryshkino. Eberbach planned to make a major push up the highway with his *Kampfgruppe* the next morning, but virtually no other Second Panzer Army units would be in a position to reinforce 4th Panzer Division for several days.

Early on 6 October, Eberbach moved the bulk of his *Kampfgruppe* up the Orel–Tula highway towards the Lisiza River crossing. The Soviet defences guarding the bridge appeared weak – merely a thin screen of NKVD troops with a few 45mm anti-tank guns and mortars. Around 0900hrs, Eberbach's artillery – a battalion of 105mm howitzers and a battery of 10cm sK18 guns from the corps-level II/AR.69 – started a brief artillery preparation against the defenders, as well as laying some smoke over the crossing site. A few minutes later, the motorcycle infantry of Kradschützen Battalion 34 seized the bridge and scattered the handful of Soviet infantry in the vicinity. Eberbach immediately pushed several companies of tanks across the bridge and they moved to secure the next ridge overlooking the crossing site. In order to protect the crossing site, Eberbach ordered a 10cm sK18 gun and two 88mm flak guns from 1st Battery, 11th Flak Battalion, to cross the Lisiza River bridge and establish overwatch positions on the far side. At first, it seemed to Eberbach that the Soviets had melted away once again, but he was wrong. Two panzer companies had just crested the ridge when they came under fire from Soviet 76.2mm tank guns from both their left and right flanks. Colonel Katukov had a company of T-34s and a few KV-1s deployed in wooded ambush positions on each side of the road and opened fire at a range of about 500m. In short order, the T-34s 'brewed up' several German PzKpfw III tanks, whose own short 50mm guns were totally ineffective against heavy tanks beyond a few hundred metres. The German tanks fell back, hoping to draw the Soviet armour upon their own concealed artillery positions. Katukov ordered his armour to pursue the retreating Germans and although the 88mm guns knocked out two T-34s, the Soviet tanks quickly overran both. As the German advance guard pulled

back across the bridge, the lone sK18 10cm gun opened fire with armour-piercing rounds and knocked out several more tanks before it too was destroyed. Katukov made the mistake of closing the range and this allowed the Germans on the south side of the bridge to knock out more Soviet tanks with point-blank fire before the Soviets withdrew up the hill. Although Guderian claimed that the 4th Panzer Division suffered 'grievous losses' in this action, the division lost 10 tanks whil personnel losses were only 7 killed and 25 wounded. According to the Germans, Katukov's brigade lost 10 heavy and 7 light tanks, although the actual number was probably half that.

After this tactical setback, Guderian decided to be more cautious in pushing up the Orel–Tula highway. German reconnaissance units crossed the Lisiza River again on 7 October and once the main Soviet defensive line was located, artillery and air attacks were used to pound these positions. By late afternoon on 7 October, Lelyushenko decided to withdraw to his next defensive position several kilometres back, since the Germans were slowly working some infantry around his right flank. Both sides spent 8 October preparing for a major battle just south of Mtensk, although Geyr von Schweppenburg was not sanguine about the chances for his depleted and poorly supplied corps to break through the Soviet defences. The first snow of the season had fallen on the night of 7 October, turning the dirt roads to mud and thereby further aggravating the poor logistic situation of Second Panzer Army.

Guderian realized that he was losing the initiative between Orel and Mtensk, his spearhead having slowed to a crawl. The Luftwaffe was able to provide 4th Panzer Division with Stuka support for the main attack on 9 October, and the Germans massed a fairly large artillery force (41 howitzers and 13 *Nebelwerfern*) to suppress the Soviet infantry. Kampfgruppe Eberbach succeeded in turning the flank of Lelyushenko's main line of resistance, precipitating a somewhat disorderly withdrawal to the outskirts of Mtensk. The Soviets failed to cover all the entrances in Mtensk and on the morning of 10 October, motorcycle infantry from

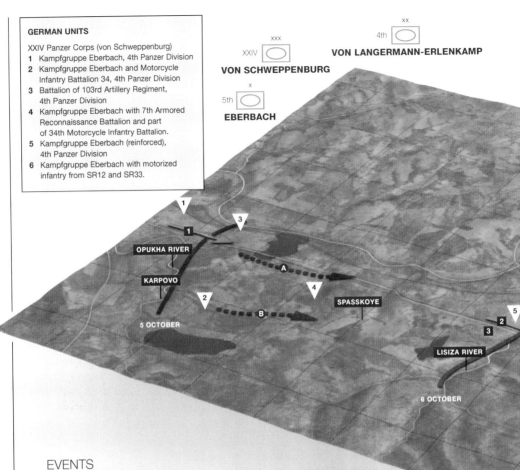

GERMAN UNITS

XXIV Panzer Corps (von Schweppenburg)
1 Kampfgruppe Eberbach, 4th Panzer Division
2 Kampfgruppe Eberbach and Motorcycle Infantry Battalion 34, 4th Panzer Division
3 Battalion of 103rd Artillery Regiment, 4th Panzer Division
4 Kampfgruppe Eberbach with 7th Armored Reconnaissance Battalion and part of 34th Motorcycle Infantry Battalion.
5 Kampfgruppe Eberbach (reinforced), 4th Panzer Division
6 Kampfgruppe Eberbach with motorized infantry from SR12 and SR33.

XX
4th

VON LANGERMANN-ERLENKAMP

XXX
XXIV

VON SCHWEPPENBURG

X
5th

EBERBACH

OPUKHA RIVER

KARPOVO

5 OCTOBER

A

B

SPASSKOYE

4

LISIZA RIVER

5
2
3
6
E

6 OCTOBER

EVENTS

1. 3 OCTOBER 1941: **Kampfgruppe Eberbach** of 4th Panzer Division occupies Orel, but the division is critically short of fuel and ammunition and must spend the next several days waiting for its supply to catch up. The Soviet 201st Airborne Brigade arrives by air transport in Orel as the German 4th Panzer Division is entering the town. The Soviets paratroopers link up with an NKVD rearguard in northern Orel and establish a blocking position on the Orel–Tula highway near Ivanovskaia.

2. 4 OCTOBER 1941: while German XXIV Panzer Corps refuels and rearms in Orel, 4th Tank Brigade sends two battle groups toward Orel to link up with NKVD rearguard.

3. 5 OCTOBER 1941 (MORNING): **Kampfgruppe Eberbach** (including 34th Motorcycle Infantry Battalion and part of the 7th Armored Reconnaissance Battalion) advances out of Orel and pushes back the weak Soviet rearguards. The Soviet tanks are able to inflict some losses on the German tanks but retire due to concentrated artillery fire from the 103rd Artillery Regiment.

4. 5 OCTOBER 1941 (NIGHT): **NKVD and 4th Tank Brigade** elements withdraw to Naryshkino to set up new defensive line. A battalion of the 11th Tank Brigade also arrives at the new position. A forward screen line is established on the Lisiza River.

5. 6 OCTOBER 1941, 0900HRS: **Kampfgruppe Eberbach** attacks the Soviet screen on the Lisiza after a brief artillery preparation. The Germans seize the bridge intact and push five companies of tanks and the 34th Motorcycle Infantry Battalion across to seize the crest of the ridgeline on the opposite side. The Germans attach two 88mm flak guns to their advance guard and overwatch the crossing with a battalion of the 103rd Artillery Regiment.

6. 6 OCTOBER 1941, 1130HRS: **Katukov's** 4th Tank Brigade launches a counterattack against the German advance guard from two directions simultaneously. The two German 88mm guns are quickly destroyed and the Soviet T-34 and KV-1 tanks begin an unequal long-range gunnery duel with the outgunned German tanks. The German advance guard pulls back toward the bridge, covered by a single sK18 10cm gun firing armor-piercing rounds in direct lay. The Soviets recklessly charge the bridge and close the range, which allows the German tanks to inflict some losses before they retire across the Lisiza River. Kampfgruppe Eberbach lost eight to ten tanks and a number of trucks and AT guns. The Soviets lost only two T-34s destroyed and four more disabled. The first snowfall occurs that night.

7. 7 OCTOBER 1941 (MORNING): **more wary of the 4th Tank Brigade after its reverse, 4th Panzer Division decides to outflank the main Soviet defensive position around Naryshkino. A mixed group of motorcycle infantry and armored cars crosses the Oka River and envelopes the right flank of the main Soviet line.**

8. 7 OCTOBER 1941 (AFTERNOON): **the Soviets withdraw 5km to the north under** cover of a barrage from two *Katyusha* rocket battalions. Lacking sufficient combat power, XXIV Panzer Corps elects to conduct reconnaissance and more air strikes on 7–8 October, but does not move up to the new Soviet positions.

9. 9 OCTOBER 1941: **Kampfgruppe Eberbach** attacks in force and achieves a breakthrough on the left flank of the new Soviet defensive line, furthest from the 4th Tank Brigade's positions. A mixed battle group of motorized infantry from SR12 and SR33 attacks near Dumchino and also achieves a breakthrough. During the night of 9/10 October, the Soviets withdraw to a final defensive position south-west of Mtensk.

10. 10 OCTOBER 1941 (MORNING): **Kampfgruppe Eberbach attacks and envelops the Soviet left flank and captures a highway bridge over the Zusha River. The Germans fight their way into the eastern side of the city and threaten to cut off the Soviet defenders south of the river.**

11. 10 OCTOBER 1941 (NIGHT) **Katukov's 4th Tank Brigade and supporting infantry withdraw from Mtensk under heavy pressure across the railway bridge on the west side of the town.**

SOVIET DELAYING ACTION AT MTENSK

5–10 OCTOBER 1941, viewed from the south showing the series of German attacks by XXIV Panzer Corps and the delaying actions of the Soviet 1st Guards Rifle Corps. This action seriously delayed Guderian's advance on Tula and demonstrated the superiority of the T-34 tank.

Note: Gridlines are shown at intervals of 3km

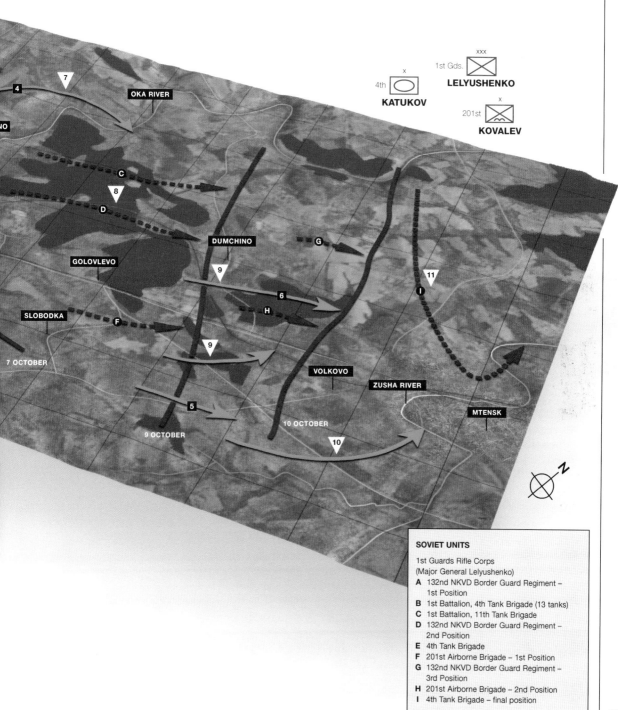

SOVIET UNITS

1st Guards Rifle Corps
(Major General Lelyushenko)

A 132nd NKVD Border Guard Regiment –
   1st Position
B 1st Battalion, 4th Tank Brigade (13 tanks)
C 1st Battalion, 11th Tank Brigade
D 132nd NKVD Border Guard Regiment –
   2nd Position
E 4th Tank Brigade
F 201st Airborne Brigade – 1st Position
G 132nd NKVD Border Guard Regiment –
   3rd Position
H 201st Airborne Brigade – 2nd Position
I 4th Tank Brigade – final position

Kampfgruppe Eberbach pulled their usual stunt – capturing a bridge intact and infiltrating Mtensk. Sensing that they were about to be cut off, Katukov withdrew his rearguards across a railroad bridge and joined the new defensive line on the north side of the Zusha River. Mtensk had fallen, but Lelyushenko had wisely used the week following the fall of Orel to construct a new defensive line on the Zusha River. Guderian's army was stopped dead on the road to Tula and made no further progress towards Moscow for the next two weeks. Guderian had lost the initiative.

THE BATTLE OF THE POCKETS AND THE PURSUIT

Army Group Centre began the battle of the Vyazma Pocket in earnest on 7 October with XL, XLVI and LVI Panzer Corps holding the eastern side of the pocket with six panzer and one motorized divisions. Sixteen infantry divisions from V, VII, VIII, IX and XXVII Corps closed in on the pocket from the west. The Soviet forces within the pocket comprised about 400,000 troops from the 16th, 19th, 20th and 32nd Armies. Before Konev left the pocket, he charged Boldin with organizing a breakout attempt to the east. Von Bock's intent was merely to crush the pocket rapidly and then pursue any remaining Soviet units east on the Moscow–Minsk highway. When the pocket was first formed, it measured about 75 by 35km, but after three days of fighting it had been reduced to about 20 by 20km. Boldin was able to escape the pocket with about 85,000 troops, but these had lost most of their equipment. Unlike the battle of the Smolensk Pocket in July, the Vyazma Pocket was sealed efficiently and there was no chance of outside aid. Army Group Centre used artillery and Stuka attacks to methodically smash everything within the pocket. The lack of any decent defensive terrain or effective leadership precluded those trapped within the pocket from forming a viable defence and Soviet morale cracked very quickly. The battle of the Vyazma Pocket was effectively over by 12 October, although mopping up continued for several more days. As a result of the battle, the Soviet Western and Reserve Fronts had lost 25 rifle divisions and five tank brigades.

Meanwhile, the Soviet Bryansk Front was also engulfed in a series of pocket battles around Bryansk. Major General Mikhail Petrov's 50th Army was loosely encircled at Lyubokhna north of Bryansk by 8 October, although Guderian only had part of the 18th Panzer Division and the 112th Infantry Division holding the east side of the pocket. On 9 October, Petrov led a partly successful breakout effort to the north-east through the weak 18th Panzer Division screen, although he was killed in the effort. The Soviets lost another five rifle divisions in the Bryansk Pocket, but parts of two divisions were able to escape. Farther south, Major General Iakov Kreizer's 3rd Army and Major General Gorodniansky's 13th Army were isolated around Trubchevsk. The terrain was fairly swampy in this area and the Germans had very little infantry to form a proper pocket. Instead, Guderian was satisfied to cut off the escape route for these 14 Soviet divisions with the 29th Motorized Division until XXXV Corps arrived to reduce the pocket. However, the German 1st Cavalry Division failed to keep a close watch on the

A Waffen-SS MG34 team in position under a railcar. On 16 October 1941, the SS Reich Division fought the Soviet 32nd Rifle Division for control of the Borodino train station. (Nik Cornish at Stavka)

encircled Soviet troops and large numbers of infantry began shifting eastward. On 11–13 October, the trapped Soviet 3rd and 13th Armies launched a major attack to break out of the Trubchevsk Pocket and they succeeded in penetrating the loose cordon of XLVII Panzer Corps. Finally, Guderian shifted forces towards Trubchevsk and the last Soviet troops inside the pocket surrendered on 20 October, but parts of at least seven of the 12 rifle divisions escaped to join the Soviet Southwest Front. The Bryansk Front had lost 12 of its 25 rifle divisions and about 110,000 troops in the first two weeks of Typhoon.

Von Bock claimed that Army Group Centre captured 673,098 prisoners, 1,277 tanks and 4,378 artillery pieces within the Vyazma–Bryansk Pockets, and another 300,000 Soviet troops were killed. Tens of thousands more troops were wounded or scattered to the four winds, leaving the Soviets badly outnumbered on the Moscow axis until reinforcements could arrive. It is certain the Western, Reserve and Bryansk Fronts lost 50–80 per cent of their troops, 97 per cent of their armour and 80 per cent of their artillery in the pocket battles. However, it was significant that eight out of nine Soviet cavalry divisions survived.

Some historians have suggested that the *Kessel* or pocket battles 'wore out' the Wehrmacht in a series of attritional battles but German losses during the battle of the Vyazma Pocket were not excessive. Colonel General Ruoff's V Corps suffered 743 killed, 2,720 wounded and 88 missing during the period 2–14 October (a loss rate of about 7 per cent). During the same period, V Corps captured 19,882 prisoners, 133 tanks, 322 artillery pieces and six *Katyusha* multiple rocket launchers. At the conclusion of the Vyazma fighting, V Corps still had almost 80 per cent of its personnel. Furthermore, German equipment losses during the Vyazma fighting were negligible.

After the Vyazma catastrophe, what remained of the Soviet Western and Reserve Fronts? The Western Front's 22nd and 29th Armies on the right of the Soviet line escaped the initial panzer *Schwerpunkt* by Third Panzer Army and began withdrawing towards Rzhev once it became clear that their neighbouring armies had collapsed. However, these two

An SdKfz 10/4 halftrack operating on the Minsk–Moscow highway in autumn 1941. Each motorized Panzerjäger battalion had a platoon of four SdKfz 10/4 halftracks with a single 20mm gun. (Nik Cornish at Stavka)

armies had only ten rifle divisions, with no armour or cavalry; their ability to conduct a counterattack was negligible. Dovator's cavalry group was able to withdraw towards the north-east, although most of its armour was lost in the initial counterattacks. Thus, Western Front's remaining forces after Vyazma were mostly infantry and reduced cavalry units, none of which were in a position to block a direct German advance on Moscow. Marshal Budenny's Reserve Front was in even worse shape, with half its divisions in the pocket and the other half scattered. Many of Budenny's divisions were militia divisions and most of these appear to have disintegrated on contact with the enemy.

Beginning on 8 October, both sides took the opportunity to re-evaluate the campaign. The German OKH was astounded by the ease with which the Soviet front had been broken and some officers believed that it was time to revise Typhoon's goals. The original objective – encirclement and destruction of the Soviet Western and Bryansk Fronts – had been achieved. What now? Given the huge Soviet losses a few weeks before at Kiev, it now seemed to the OKH that the collapse of the Soviet Union was imminent. Soviet resistance in front of Army Group Centre was now virtually non-existent. Colonel General Franz Halder, the OKH chief, advocated using this golden opportunity to roll up the Soviet Northwestern and Southwestern Fronts, and then take Moscow. The scale of the impending Vyazma–Bryansk victories impressed Hitler and he allowed the OKH to issue a number of operational directives directly to von Bock. The Ninth Army and Third Panzer Army were directed to send strong forces towards Rzhev and then Kalinin in order to cause this remaining fragment of the Soviet line to collapse. In the south, Guderian was ordered to send his XLVIII Panzer Corps towards Kursk. Obviously, the enticing vision of easily overrunning more Soviet cities was driving the OKH, but these changes served to significantly dilute Army Group Centre's main effort. On the Soviet side, Shaposhnikov realized that the Soviets had to rebuild a front line quickly if there was to be any chance of preventing a collapse. Although a large number of divisions were already en route from RVGK reserves, the shortage of rail transport meant that Zhukov would need to

A Soviet BM-13 *Katyusha* rocket launcher destroyed by air attack. The weapon was introduced in July 1941 and it was so secret that only NKVD troops were allowed to fire it. The launcher could fire 16 132mm rockets to a maximum of 9,000m. (Nik Cornish at Stavka)

make do with what was available for the next week. A ruthless decision was made to concentrate the few remaining units at blocking positions on the most likely approaches to Moscow – Mozhaisk, Volokolamsk, Naro-Fominsk and Tula. The rest of the area in front of the capital was left virtually defenceless. On 10 October, what little assets remained of the Reserve Front were rolled into the new Western Front, under the command of General Zhukov.

The German pursuit began in fits and starts, before the Vyazma Pocket had been fully crushed. Obergruppenführer Paul Hausser's SS Reich Division from XL Panzer Corps was the only major German motorized unit that was not involved in the Vyazma fighting and it was ordered to proceed eastward on the Minsk–Moscow highway. By 1230hrs on 9 October, the division's Deutschland motorized infantry regiment had captured Gzhatsk, only 175km from Moscow. However, SS Reich would have no significant reinforcement until the rest of XL Panzer Corps finished with the Vyazma fighting. Hausser decided to probe cautiously down the Minsk–Moscow highway towards Mozhaisk, with his motorcycle infantry battalion and the Der Führer Regiment. Shaposhnikov had dispatched the 18th and 19th Tank Brigades down the highway to act as a blocking force and they established a strong position in a wooded area 10km east of Gzhatsk, near the village of Budayevo. Both brigades had been raised in the last few weeks and were inexperienced, but they were equipped with three KV-1s, 34 T-34s and 63 BT-5/7s. Around 1630hrs on 9 October, Hausser's motorcycle troops ran into the blocking position and came under heavy fire from tanks and dug-in infantry. The next morning, Hausser launched the Der Führer at the roadblock, but the regiment was repulsed with about 500 casualties. The SS Reich Division was fairly weak in anti-tank capability with only two batteries of StuG III assault guns plus about six 50mm anti-tank guns to deal with 22 T-34s and 31 BT-7 light tanks in the 18th Tank Brigade. The lack of armour had caused the German spearhead towards Moscow to be stopped by only two battalions of Soviet tanks. Hausser immediately requested that XL Panzer Corps dispatch armour to support him and a panzer *Kampfgruppe* from the 10th Panzer Division was duly dispatched to Gzhatsk.

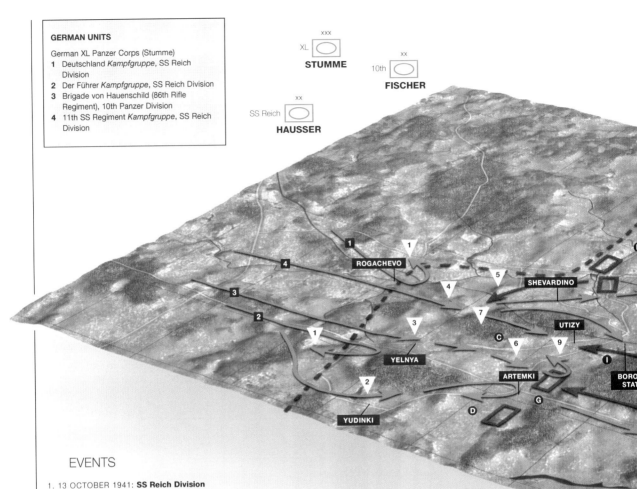

EVENTS

1. 13 OCTOBER 1941: **SS Reich Division** advances to contact with two regiments abreast down Moscow and Minsk highways. The Deutschland *Kampfgruppe* (with an attached panzer battalion from 10th Panzer Division) attempts to seize crossing over Kolotchy River near Rogachevo but is repulsed by strong defensive fires. The Der Führer *Kampfgruppe* runs into strong Soviet anti-tank defences and obstacles near Yelnya and is also repulsed after losing six tanks.

2. 14 OCTOBER 1941: **the Der Führer *Kampfgruppe* attacks Yudinki** in order to turn the flank of the 17th Rifle Regiment at Yelnya. The 2nd Battalion, Lenin Cadets, is overrun and the SS infantry push toward Artemki, which is briefly captured.

3. 14 OCTOBER 1941: **Brigade von Hauenschild** of the 10th Panzer Division arrives along the Minsk highway and launches a combined arms frontal assault on Yelnya. The German motorized infantry succeed in seizing the village but not the high ground beyond it.

4. 14 OCTOBER 1941: **After the Deutschland *Kampfgruppe* seizes a crossing over the Kolotchy River at Rogachevo,** the battle group, reinforced by the newly arrived 11th SS Regiment conduct a major drive east that penetrates the defences of the 17th Rifle Regiment and seizes Utizy. The 32nd Rifle Division begins to crumble.

5. 14 OCTOBER 1941: **the 32nd Rifle Division launches hasty counterattacks** with the division's reconnaissance battalion, anti-tank units and a few tanks from the depleted 18th and 19th Tank Brigades. Before the SS infantry can consolidate in Utizy or Artemki, they are pushed out by the Soviet counter-attack. The 322nd Rifle Regiment, finally arrived, launches a flank attack near Shevardino that throws the SS Reich Division almost back to its start line.

6. 15 OCTOBER 1941: **the Deutschland *Kampfgruppe* finally drives the remnants** of the 17th Rifle Regiment out of the high ground east of Yelnya and pushes toward Artemki, but SS Reich commander Obergruppenfuhrer Hausser is seriously wounded in Yelnya. Oberfuhrer Bittrich assumes command of SS Reich.

7. 15 OCTOBER 1941: **Brigade von Hauenschild advances** to clear the Soviets from the north side of railway line and succeeds in penetrating the main Soviet defensive belt. Major General Lelyushenko organizes a hasty counterattack that restores the line, but he is seriously wounded and replaced by Major General Govorov.

8. 16 OCTOBER 1941, 0630HRS: **with all of its units arrived, 10th Panzer Division launches** a coordinated effort to penetrate the main Soviet defensive belt. Brigade von Hauenschild attacks and seizes Borodino Station but is thrown out by a counterattack by 1st Battalion, 322nd Rifles. Von Bulow's 69th Rifle Regiment almost succeeds in reaching the 32nd Rifle Division's command post near Borodino but is stopped in desperate fighting.

9. 16 OCTOBER 1941: **the Deutschland *Kampfgruppe* advances east and seizes** Artemki, but is pushed out by a counterattack by the 20th Tank Brigade.

10. 17 OCTOBER 1941, 0630HRS: **von Bulow's 69th Rifle Regiment attacks and achieves a** breakthrough in the lines of the weakened 322nd Rifle Regiment. The spearhead of 10th Panzer captures Tatarino on the Moscow highway.

11. 17 OCTOBER 1941, 1500HRS: **the Deutschland *Kampfgruppe* finally clears** Artemki of Soviet defenders and cautiously advances a few kilometres east along the highway.

12. 17–18 OCTOBER 1941, NIGHT: **322nd Rifle Regiment falls back** toward reserve positions north of Kukarino, while remnants of the Vorobiev detachment of 32nd Rifle Division falls back along the Minsk highway.

13. 18 OCTOBER 1941: **10th Panzer and SS Reich advance upon Mozhaisk** as the 32nd Rifle Division's resistance crumbles. After heavy fighting in the outskirts of the city, two battalions of the Deutschland *Kampfgruppe* move into the city by 1500hrs.

14. 18 OCTOBER 1941, LATE: **the motorcycle Battalion from SS Reich probes** down the Minsk highway and finds minimal Soviet resistance. The battalion pushes several kilometres east of Mozhaisk.

GERMAN ASSAULT AT BORODINO

13–18 October 1941, viewed from the south showing the German XL Panzer Corps attack on the Mozhaisk Line and the stubborn defense by the Soviet 5th Army.

Note: Gridlines are shown at intervals of 3km

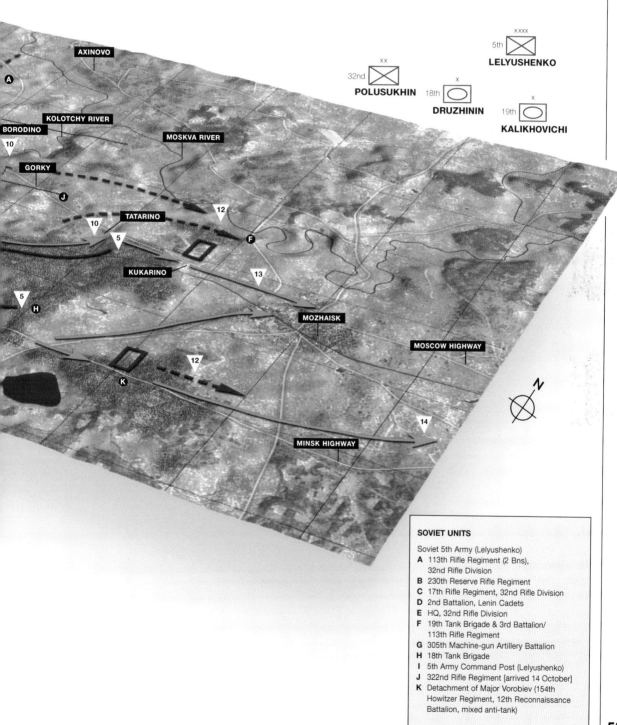

5th LELYUSHENKO (xxxx)

32nd POLUSUKHIN (xx)

18th DRUZHININ (x)

19th KALIKHOVICHI (x)

AXINOVO

A

KOLOTCHY RIVER

MOSKVA RIVER

BORODINO

10

GORKY

J

10

TATARINO

12

5

F

KUKARINO

13

5

H

MOZHAISK

MOSCOW HIGHWAY

12

K

14

MINSK HIGHWAY

N

SOVIET UNITS

Soviet 5th Army (Lelyushenko)
- **A** 113th Rifle Regiment (2 Bns), 32nd Rifle Division
- **B** 230th Reserve Rifle Regiment
- **C** 17th Rifle Regiment, 32nd Rifle Division
- **D** 2nd Battalion, Lenin Cadets
- **E** HQ, 32nd Rifle Division
- **F** 19th Tank Brigade & 3rd Battalion/ 113th Rifle Regiment
- **G** 305th Machine-gun Artillery Battalion
- **H** 18th Tank Brigade
- **I** 5th Army Command Post (Lelyushenko)
- **J** 322nd Rifle Regiment [arrived 14 October]
- **K** Detachment of Major Vorobiev (154th Howitzer Regiment, 12th Reconnaissance Battalion, mixed anti-tank)

53

A German PzKpfw 38(t) tank pulls out a bogged German staff car during the muddy period of late October 1941. The mud in Russia was a major problem for German wheeled vehicles. (Nik Cornish at Stavka)

For four days, the 18th and 19th Tank Brigades conducted a series of tenacious delaying actions on the Minsk–Moscow highway, falling back a few kilometres whenever the Germans threatened to outflank their position. However, Hausser received considerable Stuka close air support and a powerful *Kampfgruppe* from 10th Panzer, which enabled SS Reich to advance about 10km per day eastward on the highway. By 13 October, the Soviet tank brigades had lost 75 per cent of their armour and were pulled back into reserve but they had bought Zhukov precious time to get other combat units to the Mozhaisk fortified area. On 11 October, Stavka recalled Major General Lelyushenko from Mtensk and ordered him to proceed to Mozhaisk to take command of the new 5th Army. Lelyushenko was ordered to defend a 40km front with a force that initially consisted of only one infantry regiment, several separate battalions, and a few anti-tank and anti-aircraft battalions. However, on 10 October the first trains carrying the lead elements of the 32nd Rifle Division began arriving in the Mozhaisk train station from Siberia. Unlike most Soviet rifle divisions in October 1941, the 32nd Rifle Division was a full-strength unit with 15,000 trained troops. Although the division arrived piecemeal over a period of a week, it was easily the steadiest formation left between the Germans and Moscow. Lelyushenko was able to hustle two regiments of the 32nd Rifle Division into the fortified positions around Borodino and Yelnya by 13 October, just before the German advance guard arrived. However, the Luftwaffe had spotted the arrival of the 32nd Rifle Division and Hausser was prepared to launch a deliberate assault upon the Mozhaisk Line defences with the forces he had available before even more Soviet reinforcements arrived.

In addition to the main drive up the Minsk–Moscow highway, the German pursuit was able to gain ground on a broad front. Most accounts of the Moscow campaign depict the period after the first snowfall on 7 October until 15 November – the so-called *rasputitza* or mud period – as a time when the German forces were virtually immobilized but this is simply not true. After the Soviet centre gave way and XL and XLVI Panzer Corps turned northward to envelop Vyazma, General Adolf

Kuntzen's LVII Panzer Corps continued up the Moscow–Warsaw highway and captured Medyn on 11 October and reached the outskirts of the Maloyaroslavets fortified area the next day. In order to secure the flank of Fourth Panzer Army's thrust, three German infantry corps advanced fairly rapidly from the Desna to the Oka River. On 12 October, General Hans-Gustav Felber's XIII Corps captured the city of Kaluga, while General Walter Schroth's XII Corps also secured a crossing over the Oka; each corps had advanced between 70–80km in five days, despite muddy roads. Heinrici's XLIII Corps, although partly tied up with crushing the Bryansk Pocket, was able to divert a *Kampfgruppe* to seize the vital rail junction at Sukhinici on 7 October.

In the northern part of Army Group Centre's area of operations, part of Third Panzer Army and Ninth Army turned to the north-east to pursue the remnants of the Western Front. General Albrecht Schubert's XXIII Corps and General Förster's VI Corps, with a total of six infantry divisions, pursued the retreating Soviet 22nd, 29th and 31st Armies towards Rzhev. Although the Soviets had elements of 15 rifle divisions arrayed around Rzhev, the command structure was extremely jumbled, with these divisions from five different armies and no effective higher command at this point. While the German infantry pinned the Soviet infantry to the west of Rzhev, Third Panzer Army sent the 1st Panzer Division and the Lehr 900 Motorized Brigade to envelop from the south-east and they were able to capture Rzhev on 13 October. The Germans were also able to encircle most of Major General Khomenko's 30th Army south of Rzhev and destroy it. Before the Soviets could even react to this latest disaster, 1st Panzer Division pushed rapidly north-east through Staritsa to capture Kalinin, a city of 216,000, by 1645hrs on 14 October. Despite muddy roads, 1st Panzer Division was able to advance 75km in five days. The Soviet 22nd and 29th Armies fell back in confusion, with the German VI Corps pressing northward on their heels from Rzhev. The German thrust to Kalinin was amazing in its audacity, in that a single panzer division had pushed deep into Soviet lines and threatened to split the Northwestern and Western Fronts. However, the OKH had made a serious operational error in diverting part of Third Panzer Army away from Moscow in order merely to chase scattered Soviet infantry units. By 15 October, 1st Panzer Division was advancing towards Torshok – i.e. moving away from Moscow! The forces dispatched to Kalinin were insufficient to achieve a decisive victory on their own, but the diversion seriously weakened the main push on Moscow and forced the Third Panzer Army to devote significant resources to a protracted attritional fight around Kalinin. If XLI Panzer Corps had pushed east towards Volokolamsk, the Germans might have been able to prevent Zhukov from establishing a new line east of Moscow.

In addition to the 32nd Rifle Division arriving from Siberia, Zhukov had only two other divisions and several partly formed tank brigades immediately available to form blocking positions west of Moscow. The 316th Rifle Division, formed in Central Asia in July, was re-routed to join Rokossovsky's recreated 16th Army at Volokolamsk on 14 October. The 312th Rifle Division was transferred from the Volkhov Front and began arriving at Maloyaroslavets between 10 and 14 October to form a new core for the decimated 43rd Army. By 15 October, when Army Group Centre finally had sufficient forces to begin its assault on the Volokolamsk–Mozhaisk–Maloyaroslavets fortified areas, Zhukov had been able to assemble elements of 18 rifle divisions and 11 tank brigades along the 50km front – an amazing achievement in only five days. However, most of these units were either decimated remnants or partly equipped and their actual combat strength was only about 90,000 troops.

THE MOZHAISK LINE IS BREACHED

The mud had not seriously impeded the German pursuit after the Vyazma encirclement, but logistical problems, changing operational priorities and command lethargy had all contributed to the failure to rush the Soviet fortified areas before they were properly manned. By 15 October, the pursuit phase had ended and Army Group Centre now had to face a new Soviet Western Front. Furthermore, von Kluge was extremely slow in moving his infantry forward to support the attack on the Mozhaisk Line, allowing most divisions to rest and resupply around Vyazma and only one of his 11 infantry divisions participated in the assault on the Mozhaisk Line.

By 15 October, Stumme's XL Panzer Corps had the bulk of the SS Reich and 10th Panzer Divisions approaching the Mozhaisk Line defences around Borodino. German probing attacks near Rogachevo and Yelnya on 14 October demonstrated that the Soviet defences were formidable enough to merit a deliberate assault. Stumme's corps had 12 motorized infantry battalions and about 100 tanks and assault guns, supported by 89 medium artillery pieces and 33 *Nebelwerfern*. Lelyushenko's 5th Army – essentially the 32nd Rifle Division plus various odds and ends – had 12 rifle battalions and about 50 tanks supported by about 50 howitzers and a *Katyusha* rocket battalion. Thus the combat ratio at Borodino was slightly better than 1:1 in the German favour, which resulted in a fairly even battle by 1941 standards. The SS Reich Division was able to eliminate a troublesome blocking position at Yelnya but the division commander, Obergruppenführer Hausser was severely wounded there when his SdKfz 253 halftrack was hit in a *Katyusha* barrage. However, the 10th Panzer

Division was able to penetrate the main Soviet defensive belt near Borodino and Lelyushenko was also badly wounded. Throughout 15 to 17 October, the 32nd Rifle Division and 20th Tank Brigade fought doggedly around Borodino and Artemki, launching repeated counter-attacks, but the defences were gradually ground down. The German 48th Pioneer Battalion destroyed numerous concrete bunkers, which were often poorly sited due to hasty construction. The Soviet 5th Army's defences finally crumbled on 18 October and the SS Reich Division was able to seize Mozhaisk itself. The SS motorcycle battalion probed down the Minsk–Moscow highway past Mozhaisk, finding little organized resistance, but XL Panzer Corps was too spent after four days of heavy fighting to launch a pursuit. Nevertheless, the German victory at Borodino sparked a panic in Moscow and the Soviet Government began evacuating to Kubyshev.

The battle of Borodino was only one part of the struggle for the Mozhaisk Line and it was certainly not the defensive victory suggested by Soviet propaganda, which claimed that the Germans suffered 10,000 casualties and lost 100 tanks in the engagement. During the period 9–19 October, XL Panzer Corps suffered 2,044 casualties, including 446 killed; SS Reich Division suffered 1,242 casualties (incl. 270 killed), 10th Panzer Division suffered 776 casualties (incl. 167 killed). The Soviet 32nd Rifle Division and 20th Tank Brigade suffered about 60 per cent losses, rendering the best parts of the 5th Army combat-ineffective. In the period immediately following the fall of Mozhaisk, with the German spearhead only 90km from Moscow, the Soviet 5th Army had only five reduced-strength rifle divisions and about 20 tanks blocking the main highway to the capital. However, the 82nd Motorized Rifle Division began to arrive from the Far East by rail on 22 October, providing the 5th Army with one full-strength unit.

At Volokolamsk, Rokossovsky's 16th Army, primarily the 316th Rifle Division, fought off XLVI Panzer Corps and V Corps from 16 to 27 October. Shaposhnikov was able to feed a few new units to Rokossovsky, such as Katukov's 4th Tank Brigade, to keep the 16th Army from crumbling. One KV-1 tank, commanded by Lieutenant Pavel Gudz from the 89th independent Tank Battalion, succeeded in disabling ten German tanks before it was knocked out. However, some of the half-trained Soviet tankers abandoned their vehicles at the first hit. By the time Volokolamsk finally fell on 27 October, the 316th Rifle Division was reduced to only 3,500 troops, but the division had delayed Fourth Panzer Army for almost two weeks. South of Mozhaisk, the Soviet 43rd Army was unable to establish as effective a defence around Maloyaroslavets and the German LVII Panzer Corps (19th and 20th Panzer Divisions, 3rd Motorized Division) was able to seize Maloyaroslavets and Borovsk by 18 October. However, the Soviet 33rd Army at Naro-Fominsk was able to prevent the Germans from exploiting their gains. By the end of October, the whole front between Volokolamsk and Maloyaroslavets settled into a relatively quiet period for the next two weeks, as both sides rushed reinforcements and supplies to their forward units. Zhukov had succeeded in delaying a direct German advance upon Moscow, but the Mozhaisk Line was entirely overrun and Army Group Centre had five panzer divisions within 100km of the capital.

2 Kampfgruppe Eberbach initially consisted of: 2nd Battalion/35th Panzer, 34th Motorcycle Battalion, 2nd Battalion/103rd Artillery and 3rd Company/79th Armoured Engineers.

WAR OF ATTRITION,
24 OCTOBER – 14 NOVEMBER 1941

t appeared that Army Group Centre had won a major victory within three weeks of the start of Typhoon, with the Soviet Western Front severely damaged and the Mozhaisk Line overrun. Poor weather and muddy roads had been a major nuisance – particularly to horse-drawn artillery and German wheeled support vehicles – but it had not stopped the German pursuit or brought Typhoon to a halt. However, logistic shortages were another matter. Fewer supply trains reached Army Group Centre's supply heads during October than were required to support continuous offensive operations and the *Eisenbahn* troops had been slow to regauge tracks close to the new front. Furthermore, the OKH's decision to divert several corps to pursue diverging operational objectives around Kalinin and Kursk had seriously weakened the drive on Moscow.

The period between 24 October and 13 November was something of an operational pause for both sides, with Army Group Centre only capable of limited offensive action until its supply situation and the weather improved. Zhukov used this period of relative respite to consolidate the jumbled structure of units arriving at the Western Front into a coherent defence and to assemble a small operational reserve to launch counter-attacks. The Germans took the time to redistribute their forces: Second Army traded its XLIII and LIII Corps to Second Panzer Army in exchange for the XXXIV and XXXV Corps, while von Weichs gave his XIII Corps to von Kluge's Fourth Army. Von Weichs also was given Guderian's weak

German infantry assemble in a wooded area in November 1941. The first shipments of winter greatcoats began to reach front-line units in late November 1941, but there were initially only enough to equip 20 per cent of the troops. (Nik Cornish at Stavka)

XLVIII Panzer Corps and charged with holding the long right flank of Army Group Centre across 200km of open steppe from Kursk (captured on 1 November) to Yelets.

Surprisingly, it was Guderian's Second Panzer Army that made the most gains in this period. XXIV Panzer Corps had spent nearly two weeks in inactivity at Mtensk, stopped cold by the Soviet defences on the Zusha River line and the lack of adequate fuel. However, this lull in Guderian's offensive caused the Stavka to believe that the threat from this direction had passed and few reinforcements were sent to rebuild the Bryansk Front. The best Soviet commanders and units, including Lelyushenko and Katukov's 4th Tank Brigade, were withdrawn from the 'quiet' Zusha River area and sent north to Mozhaisk and Volokolamsk. By 22 October, the Second Panzer Army had managed to gather a small stock of fuel and ammunition for XXIV Panzer Corps and some infantry had been released from the Bryansk area to reinforce the new attack. Beginning on 22 October, von Schweppenburg's XXIV Panzer Corps began an attack to break out of the Mtensk bridgehead, assisted by Heinrici's XLIII Corps driving east from Belev with three infantry divisions. The initial attack by 4th Panzer Division at Mtensk on 22 October failed, but 3rd Panzer Division at Bolkhov succeeded the next day in rolling up the Soviet defensive positions. Once again, Kampfgruppe Eberbach was in the lead, and its spearhead captured Chern on 24 October and Plavsk on 27 October. On 28 October, Kampfgruppe Eberbach pierced the flimsy Soviet defensive line established south of Tula and the next day mounted an unsuccessful *coup de main* on the city. A motley collection of militia, NKVD troops and anti-aircraft units was just able to hold off Kampfgruppe Eberbach long enough for the 32nd Tank Brigade to reach Tula, followed by two rifle divisions. Despite the mud and poor roads, Kampfgruppe Eberbach had advanced 120km in one week, but once again had consumed its meagre supplies.

Guderian spent the next three weeks moving the rest of his army up the Orel–Tula highway in order to launch a major attack on Tula, but he was forced to divert much of his attention and resources to dealing with his vulnerable right flank. Many of the Soviet units in the path of XXIV Panzer Corps simply retreated eastward and by early November they were

Map legend:

- Front line, 18 Nov 1941
- Front line, 30 Nov 1941
- German armour thrusts
- German infantry thrusts
- Soviet fortified lines
- Soviet counterattacks

Scale: 0 — 10 miles / 0 — 20km

1. 29 October 1941: 4th Panzer Division attempts a *coup de main* to seize Tula. Attacking with 60 tanks and two regiments of infantry, the 4th Panzer Division *Kampfgruppe* under Colonel Eberbach breaks through the flimsy defences of the 290th Rifle Division south of Tula and reaches the outer rim of the defences before it is stopped by massed anti-tank and artillery fire.

2. 30 October 1941: Guderian assigns LIII Corps the mission of protecting the eastern flank of 2nd Panzer Army's operations against Tula. The rest of the 2nd Panzer Army slowly moves up the road from Mtensk to Tula.

3. 3–13 November 1941: a major Soviet counterattack from Yefrimov with seven divisions and a tank brigade strikes German LIII Corps at Teploye, threatening to cut main supply route to XXIV Panzer Corps. Guderian is forced to send Eberbach's *Kampfgruppe* south to reinforce LIII Corps.

4. 18 November 1941: starting positions for Guderian's final attack on Tula. XXIV Panzer Corps will attempt to envelope Tula from the east with 3rd, 4th and 17th Panzer Divisions while Grossdeutschland Regiment defends the Orel–Tula highway. 296th Infantry Division secures area south of Tula.

5. 18 November 1941: Heinrici's XLIII Corps, under Guderian's control, begins to push eastward to secure Aleksin and link up with Guderian's panzers north of Tula.

6. 18 November 1941: LIII Corps is tasked to defend the north-east flank of Guderian's panzer drive but is faced with frequent local Soviet counterattacks. The German 112th Infantry Division is attacked near Uzlovaia by the Soviet 413th Rifle Division – one of only four 'Siberian' divisions on the Moscow front at that time – and is temporarily routed. LIII Corps rectifies the situation but is capable of little further offensive action.

7. 22–23 November 1941: Guderian shifts XLVII Panzer Corps elements to secure his eastern flank; 10th Motorized Division secures Yepifan and a bridge over the Don River.

8. 24 November 1941: 4th Panzer Division, with Eberbach leading advance guard, seizes Venev and defeats a Soviet cavalry-tank covering force. 17th Panzer Division follows closely behind 4th Panzer. 3rd Panzer Division covers left flank of XXIV Panzer Corps advance while 4th Panzer's 33rd Rifle Regiment protects right flank.

9. 25–27 November 1941: LIII Corps captures Stalinogorsk then crosses the Don River at Ivanozero and establishes blocking positions.

10. 27–30 November 1941: XLIII Corps and 4th Army belatedly attack from west, seizing Aleksin. However, 4th Army does not press attack against Serpukhov and shifts to defence.

11. 30 November 1941: 29th Motorized Division is ordered to advance to the north-east and cut the Kashira–Mikhailov rail line. The division is just able to reach the rail line.

12. 30 November 1941: the 17th Panzer Division is stopped short of Kashira and is forced to pull back under pressure from I Guards Cavalry Corps.

13. 2–4 December 1941: Guderian's final effort to seize Tula. While the bulk of his army is engaged in fending off Soviet counterattacks, he launches 4th Panzer and Grossdeutschland at the salient's eastern flank. Eberbach succeeds in cutting the rail line and his motorcycle battalion briefly occupies a section of the highway, but the overextended units cannot hold these positions for long.

14. 5 December 1941: On his own initiative, Guderian shifts to the defensive and orders XXIV Panzer Corps to pull back to upper Don River.

strong enough to launch local counterattacks. Guderian directed LIII Corps to secure the right flank of the vital line of communications from Orel to Tula by establishing blocking positions near Teploye and Bogorodisk. However, just as it reached the rail junction at Teploye on 3 November, the Soviet 3rd Army launched a major counterattack that attempted to sever the German line of communications to Tula. Weisenberger's LIII Corps was almost overrun by the strong Soviet counterattack – by divisions that had escaped from the Trubchevsk Pocket – and Guderian was forced to dispatch Kampfgruppe Eberbach south to restore the situation. The fighting around Teploye lasted ten days and deprived Guderian of his armored spearhead to capture Tula. Once the 3rd Army's counterattack was repulsed, Guderian ordered LIII Corps to move further east to block any Soviet attacks from Yepifan. Another Soviet counterattack, by the new 50th Army in Tula against Heinrici's XLIII Corps, tied down the remainder of Guderian's reserves from 11 to 16 November. Although the Soviet spoiling attacks failed to inflict any serious damage, much of Guderian's supplies had been consumed in the fighting and he had to delay his attempt to seize Tula until 18 November. Once again, Soviet counterattacks and supply shortages had robbed Guderian of the initiative, following German tactical successes.

VON KLUGE FAILS TO SUPPORT TYPHOON

During the period after the annihilation of the Vyazma Pocket, von Kluge's Fourth Army accomplished virtually nothing. After spending an excessive amount of time reconstituting his army around Vyazma, von Kluge moved his divisions up to the front very slowly, despite the pressing need for infantry to support the Fourth Panzer Army. The 258th Infantry Division launched a series of small probing attacks at Naro-Fominsk from 20 to 23 October but was stopped cold by the 1st Guards Motorized Rifle Division. The 1 GMRD was an experienced formation that was rebuilding in the Moscow area at the start of Typhoon, but at this point its combat strength was equal to about two battalions of infantry and one battalion of BT-7 light tanks. By 27 October, von Kluge had 11 divisions up at the front line facing the Soviet 5th, 33rd, 43rd and 49th Armies. Von Kluge held a vital 130km stretch of the front from just east of Mozhaisk to Aleksin, south of Serpukhov. Von Bock ordered the Fourth Army to develop the situation along the Nara River line but von Kluge reported that his right flank – XII and XIII Corps – were under heavy attack near Serpukhov from the Soviet 43rd and 49th Armies on 26/27 October. Convinced that the Fourth Army was under heavy pressure, von Bock allowed it to shift to a defensive posture. It is apparent now that von Kluge lied to von Bock about the scale of the Soviet attacks in order to gain permission for an operational pause,

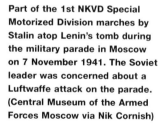

Part of the 1st NKVD Special Motorized Division marches by Stalin atop Lenin's tomb during the military parade in Moscow on 7 November 1941. The Soviet leader was concerned about a Luftwaffe attack on the parade. (Central Museum of the Armed Forces Moscow via Nik Cornish)

Two T-34/76 tanks wait in ambush in a Russian village, November 1941. Most Soviet tanks were used in small groups in infantry support roles, which reduced their operational impact. (Central Museum of the Armed Forces Moscow via Nik Cornish)

Thousands of Moscow factory workers were formed into militia units. Twelve militia divisions were sent to the front in July, but 31,000 militia were retained to garrison Moscow's fortified areas. (Central Museum of the Armed Forces Moscow via Nik Cornish)

if not an outright shift to winter quarters. An analysis of German officer casualty records for the period 26/27 October reveals that XII and XIII Corps suffered only 8 officers killed and 15 wounded in this period. Half of the casualties were in the 17th Infantry Division, with the other four divisions only lightly engaged. Despite the fact that only a single infantry division was under attack from two Soviet rifle divisions and the 20th Panzer Division was nearby in reserve, von Kluge claimed that his army was in danger and must cease any offensive actions. For the next five weeks, von Kluge allowed his front to settle into a static position, with World War I-style trenches in some areas along the Nara River. By conniving to opt out of Typhoon, von Kluge's army was the best prepared of any of Army Group Centre's formations to face the winter and the Soviet counteroffensive, but his selfish behaviour contributed to the ultimate failure of Typhoon.

The Soviet 5th and 16th Armies used this respite to fortify their new line astride the Moskva River. Further north, the Third Panzer Army and Ninth Army became involved in a protracted and useless struggle for the control of Kalinin. Konev, who had been spared from execution thanks to Zhukov, was given command of the new Kalinin Front on 17 October, which comprised the 22nd, 29th and 31st Armies, and straight away he began to counterattack. Colonel General Model's XLI Panzer Corps held a narrow salient around Kalinin and was forced to fight off repeated Soviet counterattacks from 19 to 29 October, and on 22 October Lieutenant General Maslennikov's 29th Army was able to temporarily cut the main line of communications from Staritsa to Kalinin encircling part of 1st Panzer Division. Third Panzer Army requested von Richtofen's VIII Fliegerkorps to assist the counterattacks with Stuka support and eventually the situation was stabilized around Kalinin, but the Ninth Army now had to commit most of its infantry to hold Army Group Centre's precarious left flank. The plan to link up with Army Group North was quietly abandoned.

BOTH SIDES PREPARE FOR ONE LAST EFFORT

The first phase of Typhoon had run its course by the end of October. At this point, the obvious choices were either to push on to Moscow in one last effort before the winter arrived or to shift to the defence on favourable terrain and rebuild for another offensive in the spring of 1942. Von Bock, as well as the OKH, felt that stopping the offensive when the spearheads were within 90km of Moscow was foolhardy and urged resuming Typhoon after a short period of replenishment. Hitler was unsure, as he often was in times of crisis. Although it is frequently claimed that Hitler recklessly ordered his armies to advance upon Moscow in spite of weather and supply problems, he was actually reluctant to hazard his best troops for an objective like Moscow. However, Hitler's caution was

A Soviet M1939 37mm anti-aircraft gun crew scans for German aircraft. Soviet anti-aircraft units played an important part in the ground defence of Tula and the frequent German air attacks on Moscow. (Central Museum of the Armed Forces Moscow via Nik Cornish)

FAILURE OF EBERBACH'S *COUP DE MAIN* AT TULA, 30 OCTOBER 1941 (pages 64–65)

After the fighting near Mtensk, Guderian's Second Panzer Army spent the next two weeks waiting for their supplies to catch up and for the Bryansk Pocket to be crushed. Guderian's XXIV Panzer Corps was finally able to resume its northward advance towards Moscow on 24 October. After several days of fighting, Guderian's armoured spearheads broke through the Soviet 26th Army and moved up the Orel–Tula highway towards the city of Tula. Despite the mud and poor weather Guderian's advance guard, Kampfgruppe Eberbach, was able to advance 80km in five days. Eberbach's unit, which now had about 60 tanks, several battalions of motorized infantry and an artillery battalion, reached the outskirts of Tula around 1600hrs on 29 October. However, Colonel Eberbach did not want to advance into a major urban area in the dark until he had regrouped his strung-out command; instead, he decided to wait and launch a full-scale attack into the city at first light. Inside Tula, there were very few Soviet troops to oppose Eberbach's panzers. The backbone of the Soviet defence was based on a hastily raised Workers' Militia Regiment and the 156th NKVD Regiment of the 69th NKVD Brigade, supported by the 732nd Anti-aircraft Regiment. At 0530hrs on 30 October, Eberbach began a coordinated assault on the southern approaches to Tula, with the bulk of his armour attempting to punch through the Soviet roadblocks on the highway, while his motorized infantry attempted

to flank the Soviet positions. The German PzKpfw II and PzKpfw III tanks (1) approached the roadblock on the highway and put down suppressive fire on the Soviet infantry positions but lost several vehicles to Soviet M1939 37mm anti-aircraft guns (2) firing in direct lay at the tanks. The Tula Workers Militia (3) was deployed on the left side of the highway, with a strong detachment armed with a few PTRD-41 anti-tank rifles, Maxim machine guns and Molotov cocktails. On the right side of the highway, the NKVD troops occupied a partially completed workers' housing area, which had an anti-tank ditch in front. The NKVD troops had a few 45mm M1932 anti-tank guns (4) firing at the approaching German halftracks, while snipers engaged the German infantry (5). The Germans advanced with 3rd Panzer Division's 1st Company of Schützen (Rifle) Regiment 3 in SdKfz 251 halftracks (6), supported by several companies of truck-borne infantry (7) from the Grossdeutschland Regiment. However, once the German infantry dismounted, they were pinned down in the open fields by automatic weapon fire and could not advance. German artillery and air support was minimal by this point, and the German tanks could not advance into the city unsupported. After several futile attempts that caused heavy losses among the infantry, Eberbach called off the attack. The Workers' Militia and NKVD troops had bought precious time for the defence of Tula, for the 32nd Tank Brigade arrived in Tula that night, followed shortly thereafter by three rifle divisions. While Guderian would continue to try to encircle Tula for five more weeks, his best chance had already failed.

A battery of 76.2mm F-22 USV divisional guns deployed in a wooded area, 1941. The biggest weakness of the Soviet rifle divisions in 1941 was the lack of sufficient artillery – only 16 76.2mm guns and eight 122mm howitzers were authorized. (Central Museum of the Armed Forces Moscow via Nik Cornish)

worn down by optimistic – but false – OKH intelligence estimates that depicted the Soviet forces in front of Moscow as tattered remnants, needing only one more blow to precipitate a total collapse. On 30 October, Hitler approved the OKH plan for the second phase of Typhoon, which would begin on 15 November.

By mid-October, the reinforcements ordered to the Moscow axis began to arrive and during the month of October, Zhukov received ten rifle divisions, 19 armour units, one cavalry division, five militia divisions and one airborne corps. In November, another 22 rifle divisions, 17 rifle brigades, four armour units, 14 cavalry divisions and 11 ski battalions arrived in the Moscow area. Of the initial ten rifle divisions that arrived, five went to strengthen the 5th and 16th Armies on the direct approaches to Moscow, with only two divisions sent to the Kalinin area and one to the Tula area. Although the role of the Siberians has been greatly exaggerated, Zhukov benefited from the fact that several of the units arriving from the Far East and Central Asia were pre-war units at full strength with trained troops; these divisions were extremely difficult for the Germans to dislodge once they had a chance to dig in. On the other hand, the Soviet armour units arriving at the front were of very mixed quality, both in terms of equipment and training. Several of the units consisted of cadres who picked up tanks from factories or storage depots and then went immediately to the front; such units tended to fall apart quickly in combat. In two days in November, 2nd Panzer Division captured ten T-34 tanks intact that had been abandoned by panic-stricken Soviet troops.

Zhukov expected another series of German attacks once cold weather froze the ground, so he decided to launch several small-scale spoiling attacks to disrupt the German preparations. As noted, the attacks upon Second Panzer Army succeeded in delaying Guderian's participation in the final phase of Typhoon, but most of the other attacks simply squandered precious reserves for little gain. Throughout the first half of November, the Western and Kalinin Fronts conducted brigade- and division-sized local counterattacks, which achieved little other than keeping the Germans on edge. However, Zhukov scattered his reinforcements over the entire front and thus they lacked the mass to achieve decisive results.

6th MANTEUFFEL

3 2 1

ASTRETSOVO ANDREYEVSKOYE

1

4

A

5

A

9

TEXTILE FACTORY

9

STEPANOVO

KRUGLINO

MOSKVA–VOLGA CAN.

EVENTS

1. 27 NOVEMBER 1941, 2300HRS: **an assault
group formed from the 7th Company (II/SR6,
2nd Battalion 6th Rifle Regiment) under First
Lieutenant Reineek moves from Astretsovo
into assault positions in the woods west of
Yelizavetino in order to bypass Soviet blocking
positions on the main road into Yakhroma.**

2. 28 NOVEMBER 1941, 0200HRS: **the assault
group heads south from Yelizavetino toward
the Moskva–Volga Canal, but is engaged by
enemy machineguns in Pochinki. The 133rd
Rifle Division has about a battalion-sized
rearguard covering the approaches to
Yakhroma.**

3. 0330HRS: **the assault group bypasses
the 133rd Rifle Division rearguard in Pochinki
and approaches the canal bridge at Yakhroma.
At 0410hrs, the bridge over the canal is
seized in a** coup de main **and the 40-man
Soviet security detail is captured.**

4. 0515–0545HRS: **the remainder of the 6th
Rifle Regiment and one panzer company move
quickly to reinforce the bridgehead. Soviet
artillery fire delays them around Yakhroma.**

5. 0600–1000HRS: **1st Battalion, SR6, clears
Yakhroma. The remnants of the Soviet 133rd
Rifle Division rearguard in Yakhroma retreat
southward.**

6. 0630HRS: **the rest of 2nd Battalion, SR6,
has crossed to secure the high ground east
of the canal. The Germans have only two
weak companies on the east bank.**

7. 0730HRS: **a Soviet counterattack almost
overruns the bridgehead. A Soviet tank unit
pushes down the railroad from the north and
threatens to seize the bridge.**

8. 0845HRS: **a German armored counterattack
by 11th Company, 25th Panzer, and anti-tank
guns forces the Soviets to withdraw. After
pushing the Soviets back, the regimental
commander decides to pull German armor
back to the west bank.**

9. 1000HRS: **after clearing Yakhroma, the
1st Battalion, SR6, moves across the canal
and establishes a deeper perimeter. The
2nd Battalion, SR6, pulls back across bridge
to occupy support position in Yakhroma.
3rd Battalion, 25th Panzer, is deployed
as a mobile reserve near the bridgehead.**

10. 1100–1400HRS: **Soviet infantry probes the
bridgehead from north and south and almost
penetrates the flimsy defenses but is thrown
back by German counterattacks. Soviet
bombers and artillery attack the bridge and
German troops on both sides. The textile
factory in Yakhroma is set on fire by Soviet
bombers.**

11. 1500HRS: **the Soviets hit the Germans
in Yakhroma with a heavy barrage from
Katyusha rocket launchers while launching
a major attack from the north-east to
eliminate the bridgehead. The Germans
commit their reserve, 1st Company, 6th Rifle
Regiment, and 11th Company, 25th Panzer
Regiment, to stop the attack.**

12. 2130HRS: **a Soviet attack on the east
bank from the north is successful in pushing
down between the canal and the railroad and
brings the bridge under fire. A counterattack
by the engineer platoon and 1st Company
throw them back. During a lull in the battle
in the evening, the troops dig in.**

13. 29 NOVEMBER 1941, 0230HRS: **orders
come from 7th Panzer Division to evacuate
the bridgehead. The evacuation begins
by 0500hrs and is completed by 0650hrs.
German artillery on the west bank fires
to suppress the Soviets on the east ban
as 1st Battalion, SR6, withdraws across
canal. German engineers blow a section
of the bridge to inhibit pursuit. The 6th Rifle
Regiment suffered 39 killed, 115 wounded
and 6 missing in the Yakhroma bridgehead,
a total of 160 casualties.**

THE YAKHROMA BRIDGEHEAD

27–29 November 1941, viewed from the south showing the German seizure of a bridgehead over the Moskva–Volga Canal and the Soviet counterattacks.

Note: Gridlines are shown at intervals of 1km

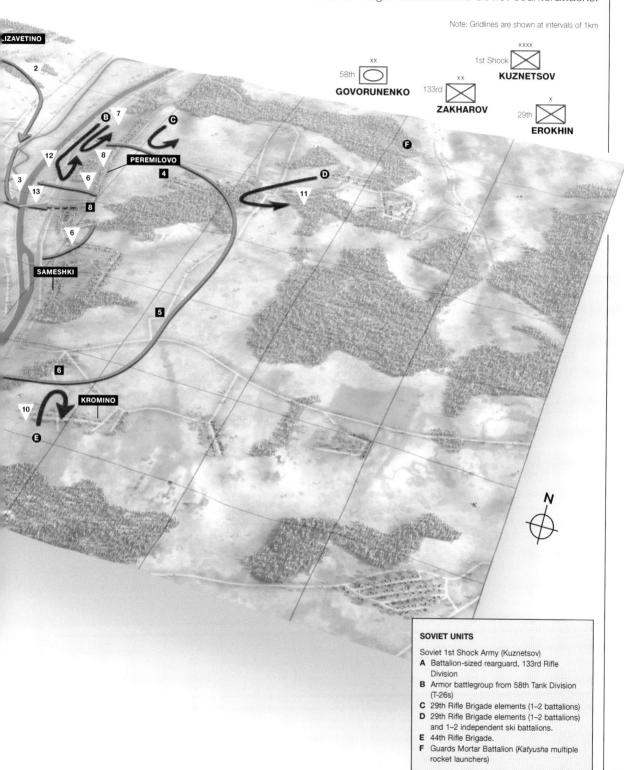

SOVIET UNITS

Soviet 1st Shock Army (Kuznetsov)
A Battalion-sized rearguard, 133rd Rifle Division
B Armor battlegroup from 58th Tank Division (T-26s)
C 29th Rifle Brigade elements (1–2 battalions)
D 29th Rifle Brigade elements (1–2 battalions) and 1–2 independent ski battalions.
E 44th Rifle Brigade.
F Guards Mortar Battalion (*Katyusha* multiple rocket launchers)

TYPHOON'S LAST GASP
15 NOVEMBER – 5 DECEMBER 1941

The German plan for the second phase of Operation Typhoon envisioned the encirclement of Moscow and the destruction of the remaining Western Front units with two powerful pincer attacks. Reinhardt's Third and Hoepner's Fourth Panzer Armies, with 18 divisions, would form the northern pincer by crushing Rokossovsky's 16th Army then establishing a bridgehead over the Moskva–Volga Canal and getting a spearhead behind the capital. Guderian's Second Panzer Army, with nine divisions, would form the southern pincer that would capture Tula and then drive north to Kolomna. While the Western Front's flanks were being smashed, von Kluge's Fourth Army would launch powerful fixing attacks along the Nara River with 14 divisions to prevent Zhukov from shifting his troops to seal off the penetrations.

Army Group Centre spent much of early November re-organizing and redistributing its forces for the next phase of Typhoon. Constant Soviet counterattacks on the flanks forced von Bock to commit all of the Second and Ninth Armies to protecting his right and left flanks, as well as distributing some armour to these vulnerable flanks. Unlike the first phase of Typhoon, Army Group Centre lacked the strength and supplies to attack along its entire front and instead had to depend upon achieving local superiority in a few areas. Third Panzer Army was particularly weakened due to the need to commit strong reserves around Kalinin and could only commit the equivalent of one panzer corps to the offensive. The real striking power was based upon Fourth Panzer Army's XL and XLVI Panzer Corps. Von Bock had a total of 36 divisions for the second phase of Typhoon – only half as many as had participated in the first phase of the offensive.

The second phase of Typhoon was further weakened by the withdrawal of much of Luftflotte 2's aircraft to other theatres, particularly the Mediterranean. By early November, von Richtofen's VIII Fliegerkorps was the only major unit left to support Typhoon, with fewer than 100 operational fighters and 200 bombers or ground-attack aircraft. The Luftwaffe's effectiveness was further reduced by poor weather and primitive maintenance facilities at the forward air bases. Thus, Army Group Centre could no longer count on much Luftwaffe support during the second phase of Typhoon. Meanwhile, the VVS had continued to rebuild from its earlier crippling losses and by mid-November the Soviets had regained local air superiority around their capital.

German logistics had not improved much despite the reduction in the operational tempo in early November. Von Bock complained that the OKH quartermaster had failed to meet Army Group Centre's quota of 30 supply trains per day for most of October and then simply cut the quota by a quarter in November, which was also not achieved. Indeed, Army Group Centre was being starved of supplies throughout much of

An abandoned T-34/76 in the winter 1941. The Soviets started the Moscow campaign with only 94 T-34/76s and most were lost in the first two weeks. By 19 November, the Stavka's tank reserve was exhausted. (Nik Cornish at Stavka)

Soviet infantry squads advancing atop KV-1 tanks in late November 1941. Instead of massing their few available KV-1s into heavy tank regiments, the Soviets reduced their impact by employing them piecemeal. (Central Museum of the Armed Forces Moscow via Nik Cornish)

A German infantry company establishing a defensive position on the edge of a village. By December 1941, most infantry companies were reduced to between 30 and 50 per cent of their authorized strength. (Nik Cornish at Stavka)

Typhoon and this prevented von Bock from amassing a logistic reserve for the renewed offensive. German *Eisenbahn* troops were able to repair the rail lines up to Gzhatsk, Volokolamsk, Kaluga and Plavsk by the start of the second phase of Typhoon, but very few supplies were actually trickling through. Most of the panzer divisions only had 1–1.5 V.S. of fuel at the start of Typhoon's second phase, which was enough for the initial attacks but not sustained operations. Furthermore, the Germans still had much of their artillery, but ammunition stockpiles were low and most would be consumed in the first few days of the offensive.

Zhukov and Shaposhnikov had achieved a near miracle in reconstituting the shattered Western Front between 10 October and 14 November, but it was questionable whether this new defensive line was strong enough to withstand a coordinated offensive. Overall, Zhukov and Konev had 53 divisions (38 infantry, three tank and 12 cavalry) and 14 tank

THE 44TH CAVALRY DIVISION ATTACKS THE GERMAN 107TH ARTILLERY REGIMENT NEAR MUSINO, 17 NOVEMBER 1941 (pages 72–73)

When the second phase of Operation Typhoon began, Marshal Zhukov ordered the Soviet 16th Army to launch hasty counterattacks to disrupt the German offensive. The 44th Cavalry Division, recently arrived on the Moscow Front from Central Asia, was sent forward to probe the German lines north of Volokolamsk. However, the Soviet cavalry commander chose to conduct the operation in broad daylight and with inadequate reconnaissance. In their path lay the German 106th Infantry Division, which had co-located a few pieces of medium artillery with each of its front-line infantry battalions. Around 1000hrs on the morning of 17 November 1941, a forward observer for the 107th Artillery Regiment spotted Soviet cavalry scouts in the woods north-east of the villages of Musino and Partenkovo. At 1130hrs, a Soviet tank platoon with four light T-26 tanks (1) moved out of the wood line and slowly advanced towards the 8th Battery, 107th Artillery, position on the north-east edge of Partenkovo. Assessing this handful of tanks as a probe, the German artillery did not give its positions away by opening fire. About 20 minutes later, more

Soviet cavalry began to appear out of the wood line north-east of Musino, about 1,300m from the German-held villages. By 1155hrs, two full Soviet cavalry squadrons (2) had formed out on the open plain and began to gallop towards Musino. The German 8th Battery on the edge of Partenkovo opened direct fire with two l.FH18 105mm howitzers (3) when the Soviet cavalry was 1km from the village and was soon joined by fire from the 7th and 9th Batteries in Musino. The German barrage disrupted the Soviet charge, but the cavalry fell back and re-formed for another effort. The Soviet regimental commander also ordered his two-gun battery of M1927 76.2mm howitzers (4) to move up and support the second attack. However, the Soviet cavalry attack fell apart under a barrage of 350 German 105mm shells, which ripped apart the lead squadrons and also disabled the horse artillery battery. The shattered Soviet cavalry fell back into the woods, having lost the bulk of a regiment. The Soviet cavalry never approached close enough to Musino for the German infantry (5) to engage them. German sources claimed that 2,000 Soviet cavalrymen died in this action and that the 44th Cavalry Division was 'destroyed' but in fact, the unit would return to exact great revenge upon the Germans under better circumstances during the Winter Counteroffensive.

brigades in the path of Typhoon's second phase, although most units were at around 60 per cent strength or less. Soviet divisions were also handicapped by severe ammunition and equipment shortages. While it would take a few months for the relocated Soviet industry to produce equipment and ammunition at full capacity, the Stavka had access to a plentiful manpower pool and it raised unit after unit and sent it to the front, often with little or no training.

Soviet intelligence detected the German preparations to renew Typhoon in mid-November and once again Stalin interfered in Stavka's planning. Stalin ordered Zhukov to launch spoiling attacks against the German Third and Fourth Panzer Armies in order to disrupt the German plans. Although reluctant to waste his small operational reserves on indecisive attacks, Zhukov was also careful to comply with Stalin's orders; the Soviet dictator had already warned Zhukov that he would pay with his life if the Germans reached Moscow. Zhukov duly ordered Rokossovsky to use his cavalry and armour to conduct spoiling attacks against Third Panzer Army by 16 November.

ROKOSSOVSKY UNDER PRESSURE

However, the second phase of Typhoon opened before Rokossovsky could act. General Alfred Wäger's XXVII Corps attacked with two infantry divisions, reinforced with an armoured *Kampfgruppe* from 1st Panzer Division, on the morning of 15 November to clear the Soviet 30th Army forces around the Moscow Sea, a dammed reservoir on the Volga River, in order to secure the flank of Third Panzer Army. The 30th Army was still recovering from the heavy fighting around Kalinin and its two divisions in this area fell back across the Volga River. In a day, Ninth Army had relieved much of the pressure from the German salient in

A Soviet ski battalion moves up to the front, late November 1941. The Soviet Western Front received 11 ski battalions, each of 400–500 troops, just before the start of the Winter Counteroffensive. (Central Museum of the Armed Forces Moscow via Nik Cornish)

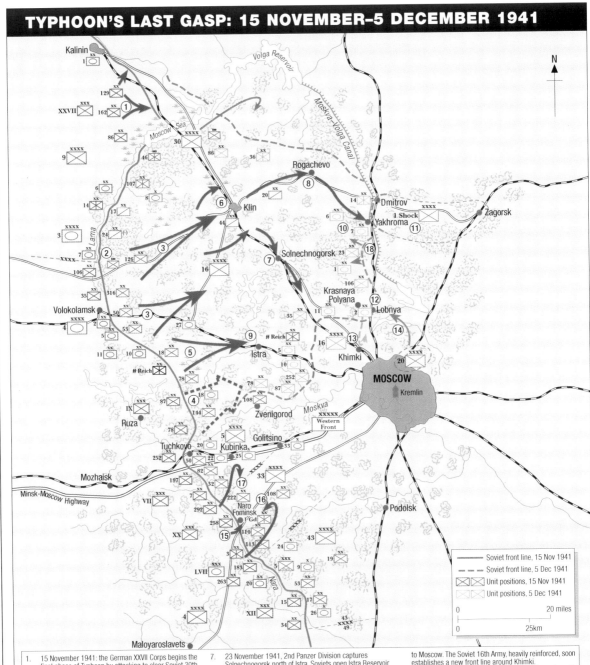

Soviet front line, 15 Nov 1941		
Soviet front line, 5 Dec 1941		
Unit positions, 15 Nov 1941		
Unit positions, 5 Dec 1941		

0   20 miles
0   25km

1. 15 November 1941: the German XXVII Corps begins the final phase of Typhoon by attacking to clear Soviet 30th Army elements around the Moscow Sea and Volga Reservoir (5th RD, 21st TB) in order to secure the flank of 3rd Panzer Army.
2. 17 November 1941: LVI Panzer Corps/3rd Panzer Army attacks and seizes a crossing over the Lama River.
3. 18 November 1941: 4th Panzer Army joins offensive with a major attack toward Klin by V Corps (35, 106th Infantry Divisions) and XLVI Panzer Corps (2nd Panzer Division). Under heavy pressure, the Soviet 16th Army begins withdrawing toward Istra and Solnechnogorsk. The German spearheads quickly create a gap between the Soviet 16th and 30th Armies.
4. 19–20 November 1941: German IX Corps attacks toward Zvenigorod to pin down Soviet 5th Army.
5. 19 November 1941: 4th Panzer Army's XL and XLVI Panzer Corps join the offensive and drive toward Istra.
6. 23 November 1941: Klin captured by LVI Panzer Corps/3rd Panzer Army after heavy fighting with 16th Army. The Soviet front west of the Moskva–Volga Canal begins to crumble.

7. 23 November 1941, 2nd Panzer Division captures Solnechnogorsk north of Istra. Soviets open Istra Reservoir and flood nearby area.
8. 24 November 1941: LVI Panzer Corps pushes east from Klin toward Rogachevo.
9. 25 November 1941: XL Panzer Corps (10th Panzer, SS Reich) reach Istra River. The Soviet 78th Siberian RD defends Istra tenaciously and the town does not fall to the SS Reich Division until 27 November.
10. 27 November 1941: 7th Panzer Division/3rd Panzer Army seizes crossing at Yakhroma over Moskva–Volga Canal but is forced to evacuate it early on 29 Nov. Both corps of 3rd Panzer Army reach canal by 30 November and spend next several days clearing Soviets on west bank.
11. 24–27 November 1941: Soviet 1st Shock Army assembles between Dmitrov, Yakhroma and Zagorsk.
12. 30 November 1941: Krasnaya Polyana falls to 2nd Panzer Division and some patrols reach the Lobnya railroad station.
13. 30 November 1941: a motorcycle patrol of 62nd Panzer Pioneer Battalion reaches Khimki, 6km from the Moscow outskirts, then withdraws. This is closest Germans reach

to Moscow. The Soviet 16th Army, heavily reinforced, soon establishes a new front line around Khimki.
14. 1 December 1941: newly formed Soviet 20th Army elements move up and create new line in vicinity of Lobnya.
15. 1 December 1941, 0500hrs: the German 4th Army belatedly joins the offensive. XX Corps attacks and breaches the Soviet 33rd Army defences, capturing Naro-Fominsk and Akulovo. LVII Panzer Corps attacks and also penetrates the Soviet defences on the Nara River.
16. 2 December 1941: Zhukov dispatches reinforcements to 33rd Army; Soviet counterattack stops 4th Army offensive near Burtsevo.
17. 3 December 1941: von Kluge calls off 4th Army offensive and begins withdrawal without orders back behind Nara River. 4th Panzer Army offensive ends.
18. 4–5 December 1941: 1st Shock Army attacks 3rd Panzer Army south-west of Yakhroma, which draws off the remaining German offensive strength.
19. 5 December 1941: all German forces shift to defensive and begin planning local withdrawals to better defensive positions.

A company of Soviet T-34/76 tanks and infantry moving up to the front. The Soviet Winter Counteroffensive was plagued by a shortage of armour and artillery and there were fewer than 150 T-34s available to the Western Front on 5 December. (Central Museum of the Armed Forces Moscow via Nik Cornish)

Kalinin while unhinging the boundary between the Kalinin and Western Fronts. On 16 November, Third Panzer Army's LVI Panzer Corps began crossing the Lama River against the left flank of the 30th Army, which was more of a screening force than a strong defensive line. The 30th and 16th Armies launched their spoiling attacks against LVI Panzer Corps' bridgehead without achieving anything.

With the Soviet 30th Army front between the Moscow Sea and Volokolamsk disrupted by the initial German attacks, Fourth Panzer Army began the main part of the offensive on 18 November by attacking eastward from Volokolamsk with Ruoff's V Corps (three infantry divisions) and von Vietinghoff's XLVI Panzer Corps (2nd, 5th and 11th Panzer Divisions), which had over 400 tanks. Hoepner's attack was intended to split the seam between the 30th and 16th Armies. Rokossovsky had argued with Zhukov for the need to employ a more elastic defence in order to rebuild his strength but Zhukov ordered that not one inch would be ceded to the Germans. Nevertheless, Hoepner's attack discovered that cavalry screens mostly held the Soviet 16th and 30th Army fronts with only three rifle divisions deployed along this 90km-wide front. Stalin's spoiling attack had only served to seriously weaken the Soviet front-line units just before the main German attack. Under pressure from five panzer divisions, the Soviet cavalry and infantry fell back towards Klin. By the evening of 18 November, Fourth Panzer Army's attack had begun to split the Soviet 16th and 30th Armies. As 30th Army fell back towards Klin, 16th Army fell back towards Istra, further opening up a gap between the two armies. Major General Lelyushenko, recovered from his wounds at Borodino, took command of the 30th Army on the night of 18 November and was ordered by Zhukov to hold Klin at all costs. With both 16th and 30th Armies in retreat, Hoepner increased the pressure on the morning of 19 November by attacking with XL Panzer and IX Corps on Rokossovsky's left flank. At the same time, von Bock ordered Ninth Army to shift completely to the defensive and hold off Konev's Kalinin Front – which began to launch a series of division-sized counterattacks – while Hoepner and Reinhardt crushed the right flank of Zhukov's Western Front. Lelyushenko arrived in Klin to find his new command in headlong retreat but he quickly established an effective defence in the city that was able to hold off the Germans for five days. Finally, the German LVI Panzer Corps cut the road to the north of Klin while V Corps cut the road to the south. On 23 November, Lelyushenko pulled his remaining troops out of Klin just as the trap was closing and pulled back towards the Moskva–Volga Canal. Reinhardt's Third Panzer Army quickly exploited the Soviet withdrawal, capturing Solnechnogorsk on 23 November and Rogachevo the next day. Probing south along the Klin–Moscow rail line, a *Kampfgruppe* from 2nd Panzer Division encountered the Soviet 146th Tank Brigade near Peshki on 25 November; this Soviet unit was equipped with British-built Matilda II tanks and was one of the first examples of Allied lend-lease equipment reaching the front.

TO THE OUTSKIRTS OF MOSCOW

Farther south, Rokossovsky's situation was equally desperate, since his army was facing the main weight of Hoepner's attack. Rokossovsky placed his best unit in the key town of Istra, the 78th Rifle Division, which had arrived from Siberia on 17 October with a full complement of troops and artillery. The terrain around Istra favoured the defence, with a large reservoir to the north of the town and marshy terrain to the south. Hoepner committed Stumme's XL Panzer Corps to a direct, frontal assault on the town. The 78th Rifle Division put up a desperate defence for three days, withdrawing on 27 November. SS Reich Division suffered 255 killed and 671 wounded in the fight for Istra, which seriously depleted the remaining infantry strength in that formation. Rokossovsky had not been able to stop Hoepner's attack, but the German offensive had begun to break down into a series of poorly coordinated corps- and division-level attacks that allowed most Soviet units to escape. By 28 November, Rokossovsky had established a new defensive line about 35km north-west of Moscow.

The fighting for Klin and Istra had consumed much of Third and Fourth Panzer Armies' supplies and incurred significant losses, while no Soviet units were encircled or destroyed. By late November the weather was becoming more than a nuisance and was seriously degrading the combat capability of the German infantry. Reinhardt's LVI Panzer Corps was able to reach the Moskva–Volga Canal at Yakhroma on 27 November and gain a bridgehead, but was unpleasantly surprised to find the lead elements of the new Soviet 1st Shock Army detraining nearby. After a brief stay on the east bank with von Manteuffel's *Kampfgruppe*, Reinhardt evacuated the bridgehead and redirected his army – in reality only four divisions – to clear the west bank of the canal in order to protect Hoepner's left flank. By 30 November, Reinhardt's army had shifted to the defence. Hoepner's army continued the offensive on its own for a few days, but its momentum was gone. The 2nd Panzer Division's rifle brigade captured Krasnaya Polyana on 30 November, 32km from the Kremlin, but the German northern pincer could advance no further, due to increasing Soviet resistance, poor weather and lack of fuel.

Despite von Bock's repeated orders to join the offensive, von Kluge's Fourth Army sat immobile on the Nara River all through November. Due to this inactivity, Zhukov was able to shift forces from the unengaged 5th and 33rd Armies to reinforce Rokossovsky's new defensive line. Instead, von Kluge played an odd waiting game and only launched his attack once Fourth Panzer Army had been stopped. At 0500hrs on 1 December, the Fourth Army's XX and LVII Panzer Corps attacked with four divisions, including 20th Panzer Division. Von Kluge's offensive was a case of too little, too late, but it was also an example of a superbly planned and executed set-piece assault. Despite the fact that the Soviet 33rd Army had spent over a month constructing thick defences around Naro-Fominsk, von Kluge's well-rested infantry cut through the main line of resistance in a matter of hours. Naro-Fominsk was captured and two German infantry divisions achieved a major breakthrough of the 33rd Army's line. Zhukov quickly shifted forces to reinforce the crumbling 33rd Army front, which launched a small counterattack on 2 December. After 48 hours, von Kluge called off the offensive and began withdrawing his forces behind the Nara River. Von Kluge's XIII Corps was also supposed to support Guderian's attack against Tula by capturing Serpukhov, but to Guderian's open disgust, von Kluge only allowed this corps to send small patrols out. On account of the fact that they had consumed fewer supplies than any of Army Group Centre's other armies and had essentially shifted to the defensive in late October, von Kluge's Fourth Army was well set to resist the Soviet Winter Counteroffensive when it came, but von Kluge had robbed Typhoon's final phase of any chance of success. Zhukov later wrote, 'in the absence of attacks at the centre we were able to shift all our reserves, down to divisional reserves, from the centre of the front to parry the enemy's strike forces on the flanks.'

GUDERIAN'S LAST TRY FOR TULA

Meanwhile, Guderian's Second Panzer Army had spent much of November fighting off Soviet counterattacks and trying to gather enough fuel to mount one last attack before winter arrived in full force. However, the Soviets were able to build up Boldin's 50th Army more quickly than Guderian could reconstitute his own combat capability and by mid-November the Soviets had six rifle and one tank division in Tula. After several small probes at the city's southern defences, Guderian decided that he would envelop Tula from the east and west rather than risk a costly frontal assault. On 18 November, the two infantry divisions of Heinrici's XLIII Corps began attacking eastward to capture Aleksin and cut the main Serpukhov–Tula highway. However, before Guderian could commit his armour, Weisenberger's LIII Corps suffered a painful counterattack at Uzlovaia by the Siberian 413th Rifle Division. Guderian was forced to spend several critical days restoring his open right flank and he had to dilute his offensive by committing two motorized infantry divisions from Lemelsen's XLVII Panzer Corps to strengthen the spent LIII Corps.

Guderian was not able to begin his offensive until 24 November, with XXIV Panzer Corps (3rd, 4th and 17th Panzer Divisions) advancing to the north-east of Tula. Kampfgruppe Eberbach was once again in the

HIGH WATER MARK OF THE WEHRMACHT,
1 DECEMBER 1941 (pages 80–81)

After the fall of Istra on 27 November 1941, the remnants of the Soviet 16th Army fell back in some disarray towards Moscow. Although Rokossovsky was able to quickly re-establish a new defensive line closer to the capital, the retreat left some temporary gaps. Fourth Panzer Army dispatched a number of patrols to try and infiltrate the threadbare Soviet lines and find a suitable crossing over the Moskva–Volga Canal – the last major water obstacle between the Germans and the Soviet capital. Around 1900hrs on 1 December 1941, a motorized patrol from the German 62nd Panzer Pioneer Battalion managed to slip unobserved through a gap in Rokossovsky's line. During the night, temperatures rose due to a thaw, creating patches of thick ground fog that aided the German infiltration and not a shot was fired at the patrol as it moved steadily closer to Moscow. Around dawn, the German patrol reached the train station in the village of Khimki, still without being fired upon. The distance from the Khimki train station to the Kremlin was 19km. Russian civilians in Khimki panicked when they saw Germans riding into the town and either hid or fled, although a few local militia members fired at the Germans from a distance. The patrol leader realized that they had discovered an unprotected route to the capital and realized that he must report this vital information quickly to Fourth Panzer Army. After a brief stay in Khimki, the German troops drove back the way they had come and reached the German lines. However, the Fourth Panzer Army no longer had the combat strength left to take advantage of this coup. The German patrol was probably built around a Motorized Light Combat Engineer Company and supposedly had about eight motorcycles plus a few light vehicles. This scene depicts the reconnaissance patrol as having several BMW motorcycles with and without sidecars (1), two Type 82 Kubelwagens (2) and one SdKfz 15 medium personnel carrier (3), along with about 20 troops. Operation Barbarossa was the first campaign for the nimble Type 82 and its good performance on poor-quality Russian roads made it an instant favourite. However, the SdKfz 15, which was often used as a scout car in engineer units, suffered during Typhoon from poor off-road capability and a weak transmission. The German lieutenant leading the patrol looks at the poster on the wall of the train station and realizes just how close they are to the Soviet capital. (4)

lead, capturing the road intersection of Venev and scattering a Soviet tank-cavalry covering force. While 17th Panzer advanced on Kashira, 4th Panzer Division and the Grossdeutschland Regiment pivoted west and attempted to cut the rail line into Tula. The initial weakness of Soviet resistance east of Tula encouraged the OKH to believe that Second Panzer Army could wreak havoc south-east of Moscow and Guderian was ordered to dispatch the 29th Motorized Division to advance eastward and cut the Kashira–Mikhailov railway line. However after a few days of advancing, Guderian's spearheads had ground to a halt as they ran into unexpectedly strong Soviet forces; 17th Panzer was stopped short of Kashira and XLIII Corps was stopped after capturing Aleksin. On 2 December, Guderian decided to make one last effort to encircle Tula and destroy the 50th Army. While the bulk of Second Panzer Army held off a number of Soviet counterattacks, Kampfgruppe Eberbach and the Grossdeutschland Regiment attacked westward and succeeded in reaching the Tula–Serpukhov railway line with some motorcycle infantry before being forced to withdraw on 4 December under heavy pressure.

By the evening of 4/5 December, all of Army Group Centre's armies had shifted to the defence. In military terms, Operation Typhoon had 'culminated', meaning the point had been reached when the attacking army was no longer stronger than the defending army. Realizing that many of the forward units were dangerously exposed and virtually out of supply, many commanders began to request permission to conduct local withdrawals to better defensive positions. Without waiting for permission, Guderian began to pull XXIV Panzer Corps back from its dangerous position north of Tula.

The second phase of Typhoon had failed to capture Moscow or to destroy any sizeable Soviet forces, but Army Group Centre remained dangerously close to the Soviet capital.

DESPERATE DAYS
5 – 15 DECEMBER 1941

Unknown to von Bock, Stalin had approved Shaposhnikov's plan for a Winter Counteroffensive on 30 November, just as the German spearheads were grinding to a halt. While Zhukov had been stabilizing the Western Front, Shaposhnikov had been slowly accumulating three new armies – the 1st Shock Army and 20th Army north of Moscow and the 10th Army near Kolomna – for a counteroffensive. These Soviet armies were not particularly strong, being especially weak in armour and artillery, but they had received substantial amounts of fresh infantry replacements just as Typhoon was culminating at the end of November. Although Shaposhnikov and Zhukov argued heatedly about just how to use these reinforcements, they did agree that the first move must be to repulse Hoepner's and Guderian's panzer spearheads.

GERMAN DISASTER IN THE KLIN BULGE

At 0300hrs on 5 December 1941, Konev's Kalinin Front began the Winter Counteroffensive by launching attacks east of Kalinin with the 31st Army. Eight hours later, the 29th Army joined in by attacking west of Kalinin. The German XXVII Corps repulsed the uncoordinated attacks by the 29th Army, but the Soviet 31st Army threatened to envelop Kalinin from the east. Both armies were able to establish small bridgeheads across the Volga River. At this point, Hitler agreed to suspend all offensive operations due to the deteriorating weather, but he ordered Army Group Centre to defend its hard-won gains.

Von Bock and Reinhardt had made critical errors that contributed to the initial success of the Soviet Winter Counteroffensive. Von Bock had stripped Reinhardt's Third Panzer of almost all its infantry divisions in order to reinforce Ninth Army's vulnerable flank around Kalinin, leaving Reinhardt with three panzer and two motorized infantry divisions in the 'Klin Bulge'. Although Reinhardt's forces had essentially shifted to the defensive after the evacuation of the Yakhroma bridgehead, he failed to pull any armour back from the Moskva–Volga Canal to create a mobile reserve and he left much of his artillery deployed close behind the front line. All three of Reinhardt's panzer divisions – which had perhaps 75–80 operational tanks on 5 December – were concentrated in the eastern tip of the bulge near Dmitrov and Yakhroma. Reinhardt's extended left flank, from Dmitrov on the Moskva–Volga Canal to Zakharovo – a distance of over 60km – was held by only the 14th and 36th Motorized Infantry Divisions. A mere screening force, not a defence, covered the flank of the German bulge.

At 0600hrs on 6 December, Lelyushenko's 30th Army attacked the two German motorized infantry divisions with three rifle divisions and

INITIAL SOVIET COUNTERATTACKS AND GERMAN WITHDRAWALS, 5-16 DECEMBER 1941

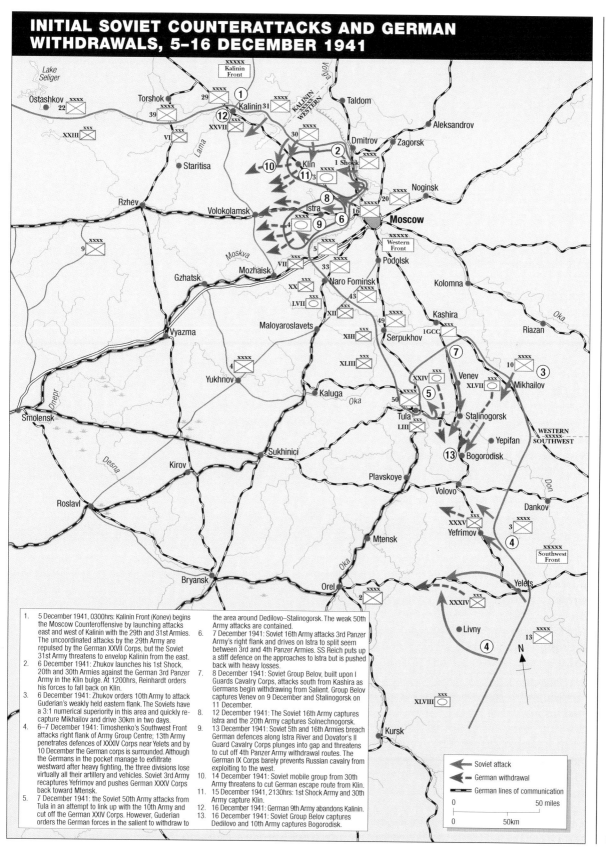

1. 5 December 1941, 0300hrs: Kalinin Front (Konev) begins the Moscow Counteroffensive by launching attacks east and west of Kalinin with the 29th and 31st Armies. The uncoordinated attacks by the 29th Army are repulsed by the German XXVII Corps, but the Soviet 31st Army threatens to envelop Kalinin from the east.
2. 6 December 1941: Zhukov launches his 1st Shock, 20th and 30th Armies against the German 3rd Panzer Army in the Klin bulge. At 1200hrs, Reinhardt orders his forces to fall back on Klin.
3. 6 December 1941: Zhukov orders 10th Army to attack Guderian's weakly held eastern flank. The Soviets have a 3:1 numerical superiority in this area and quickly re-capture Mikhailov and drive 30km in two days.
4. 6–7 December 1941: Timoshenko's Southwest Front attacks right flank of Army Group Centre; 13th Army penetrates defences of XXXIV Corps near Yelets and by 10 December the German corps is surrounded. Although the Germans in the pocket manage to exfiltrate westward after heavy fighting, the three divisions lose virtually all their artillery and vehicles. Soviet 3rd Army recaptures Yefrimov and pushes German XXXV Corps back toward Mtensk.
5. 7 December 1941: the Soviet 50th Army attacks from Tula in an attempt to link up with the 10th Army and cut off the German XXIV Corps. However, Guderian orders the German forces in the salient to withdraw to the area around Dedilovo–Stalinogorsk. The weak 50th Army attacks are contained.
6. 7 December 1941: Soviet 16th Army attacks 3rd Panzer Army's right flank and drives on Istra to split seem between 3rd and 4th Panzer Armies. SS Reich puts up a stiff defence on the approaches to Istra but is pushed back with heavy losses.
7. 8 December 1941: Soviet Group Belov, built upon I Guards Cavalry Corps, attacks south from Kashira as Germans begin withdrawing from Salient. Group Belov captures Venev on 9 December and Stalinogorsk on 11 December.
8. 12 December 1941: The Soviet 16th Army captures Istra and the 20th Army captures Solnechnogorsk.
9. 13 December 1941: Soviet 5th and 16th Armies breach German defences along Istra River and Dovator's II Guard Cavalry Corps plunges into gap and threatens to cut off 4th Panzer Army withdrawal routes. The German IX Corps barely prevents Russian cavalry from exploiting to the west.
10. 14 December 1941: Soviet mobile group from 30th Army threatens to cut German escape route from Klin.
11. 15 December 1941, 2130hrs: 1st Shock Army and 30th Army capture Klin.
12. 16 December 1941: German 9th Army abandons Kalinin.
13. 16 December 1941: Soviet Group Belov captures Dedilovo and 10th Army captures Bogorodisk.

two tank brigades, equipped with 56 light tanks. The attack began without air or artillery support, and Lelyushenko's attack was spread out over a very wide front, but his forces quickly succeeded in advancing 12km against the thinly spread 36th Motorized Infantry Division north of Klin. Kuznetsov's 1st Shock Army, which had already gained a foothold across the Moskva–Volga Canal prior to the onset of the Winter Counteroffensive, also attacked the 14th Motorized Infantry and 6th Panzer Divisions at the eastern end of the bulge with five rifle brigades. Despite its impressive title, the 1st Shock Army had no armour and very little artillery. Reinhardt's depleted forces were poorly deployed to repel any attacks, but he and his corps commanders failed to react as Lelyushenko's attack began to split the seam between the two motorized infantry divisions on 7 December. One Soviet assault group succeeded in attacking LVI Panzer Corps' headquarters at Bolshoye Shchapovo 4km north-east of Klin and General Ferdinand Schaal had to use a rifle to defend his command post. However, the German command seemed initially paralysed or apathetic about the developing threat, perhaps as a result of mental and physical exhaustion after nine weeks of continuous offensive operations; von Bock described the Soviet penetrations of Third Panzer Army's northern front as 'unpleasant'. In conjunction with the attacks by Lelyushenko and Kuznetsov, the 20th and 16th Armies began attacks on 6 December against the 2nd Panzer Division's exposed position at Krasnaya Polyana. Although Rokossovsky's army was still seriously depleted by its role in stopping the German offensive, he had enough infantry left to conduct serious fixing attacks against Fourth Panzer Army's front that prevented it from shifting any significant forces to help Reinhardt.

The situation became very unpleasant for Third Panzer Army on 8–9 December as the 30th Army's spearhead – the 8th Tank Brigade under Colonel Pavel Rotmistrov – cut the Kalinin–Klin road and captured Yamuga. The German situation in Klin was chaotic, with a hasty defence organized from anti-aircraft and support units. At the same time, the 1st Shock Army captured Fedorovka on the eastern side of the bulge and the 16th Army succeeded in pushing back the SS Reich Division towards Istra. Reinhardt finally ordered his hard-pressed panzer divisions to begin falling back towards Klin, while Hoepner ordered his forces to conform by withdrawing to the line Solnechnogorsk–Istra. As the German panzer armies began withdrawing, the Soviet 5th Army joined in the offensive. Von Bock was able to dispatch a few infantry battalions to Klin by truck, but Third Panzer Army was in serious danger of being encircled in Klin. Reinhardt used *Kampfgruppen* from the 6th and 7th Panzer Divisions to counterattack Rotmistrov's tanks at Yamuga, while pulling most of Third Panzer Army into Klin. A large amount of stranded German artillery and motor vehicles were abandoned in the hasty retreat east of Klin. Once he had his forces fairly concentrated, Reinhardt was able to hold the city but the Soviet infantry and cavalry just slipped around his left flank into the yawning gap between Third Panzer Army and Ninth Army.

Hoepner attempted to assist Reinhardt by dispatching his 10th Panzer Division to assist the defence of Klin, but the shortage of fuel and poor weather made rapid movements difficult. Rokossovsky took advantage of 10th Panzer's withdrawal to launch a frontal assault against XL Panzer Corps on 11 December that succeeded in capturing Istra while the 20th Army captured Solnechnogorsk. By this point, the entire left wing of Army Group Centre was falling back in disarray. On 12 December, Lelyushenko formed a mobile group with the 8th and 21st Tank Brigades, the 2nd Motorized Regiment, the 46th Motorcycle Regiment and two cavalry units – all under Rotmistrov – to cut off Third Panzer Army's retreat. Two days later, Rotmistrov's group cut the road out of Klin to the west, thereby isolating the 1st, 2nd, 6th and 7th Panzer Divisions plus the 14th Motorized Infantry Division. In a desperate race, XLI and LVI Panzer Corps abandoned much of their equipment and retreated to the south-west while a small rearguard held Klin. Two *Kampfgruppen* from the 1st and 2nd Panzer Divisions successfully counterattacked at Nekrasino and opened the escape route for Third Panzer Army. Klin was abandoned at 2130hrs on 15 December and Third Panzer Army was saved from encirclement but its five mobile divisions were combat ineffective after the loss of most of their heavy equipment.

Although Third Panzer Army's battle casualties were actually fairly light in the Klin Bulge, the damage to morale was tremendous. The commander of LVI Panzer Corps, General Schaal, complained that many of his troops had lost the will to fight and were simply walking towards the rear to escape the cold and possible capture. Hoepner's Fourth Panzer Army was also faced with possible encirclement as the 2nd Guard Cavalry Corps penetrated the flimsy German line near Svenigorod and threatened to wreak havoc with the rear area support troops. By 15 December, Fourth Panzer Army was falling back all along its front. Ninth Army suffered heavily in the fighting around Kalinin and by 16 December that city was back in Soviet hands.

GUDERIAN IS ROUTED

While Shaposhnikov's counteroffensive was routing Third and Fourth Panzer Armies in the north, an equally determined effort was made to put paid to Guderian's overextended Second Panzer Army. Although Guderian had issued orders to his forward units to conduct tactical withdrawals on 5 December, his army was hit by major attacks on 6–7 December by the 50th Army in Tula, the 1st Guard Cavalry Corps from Kashira and the new 10th Army, which recaptured Mikhailov. Even worse for Guderian, the 3rd and 13th Armies from Timoshenko's Southwest Front attacked the weak German Second Army on his right flank. Soviet cavalry surrounded XXXIV Corps near Livny on 10 December, and its 45th, 95th and 134th Infantry Divisions were encircled for several days and threatened with annihilation. Lieutenant General Conrad von Cochenhausen, commander of the 134th Infantry Division, committed suicide on 13 December when he feared capture was imminent. Eventually, the three German divisions escaped the encirclement – they were not destroyed as some sources claim – but they suffered very heavy personnel and equipment losses.[3] Although Guderian's XXIV and XLVII Panzer Corps were able to parry some of the initial infantry-heavy Soviet attacks, the Soviets succeeded in driving wedges between Second Panzer Army and both Second and Fourth Armies. By 12 December, both of Guderian's flanks were torn open and he had no choice but to retreat as fast as possible to the south-west. Soviet cavalry had already begun to exploit Second Army's collapse and threatened to cut the main supply line from Orel.

The initial phase of the Soviet Winter Counteroffensive had repulsed all three German panzer armies from Moscow and indeed, had thrown five out of six armies in Army Group Centre into disarray. Only von Kluge's Fourth Army, which had begun preparing its defences weeks before and stockpiling supplies, lost no significant amount of ground to the Soviet offensive. The Soviet Winter Counteroffensive has been distorted with images of masses of warmly clad Siberian troops riding into battle on hundreds of T-34 tanks but in fact, it was the Soviet cavalry that played the most significant role in the initial phase of the Counteroffensive. Zhukov, Konev and Timoshenko were only able to commit small amounts of armour in the opening attacks and most were light tanks.

---

3 The 95th Infantry Division suffered 1,088 battle casualties during 18 November–17 December, including 457 missing. The 95th also lost 13 artillery pieces and 18 anti-tank guns in this period. After the breakout from Livny, the 95th still had an average combat strength of 328 men in its six infantry battalions. The 45th Infantry Division lost almost all its artillery (31 howitzers, 44 anti-tank guns) and vehicles in the Livny Pocket.

AFTERMATH

The first phase of the Soviet Winter Counteroffensive had run its course by the end of December and Army Group Centre had been decisively repulsed in front of Moscow. Although Kaluga was lost on 26 December, both Vyazma and Rzhev remained in German hands throughout the winter. During the course of Operation Typhoon, the combat elements of Army Group Centre had suffered about 110,000 casualties, including over 24,000 killed and 5,000 missing in action. German equipment losses in December 1941 were particularly heavy, including 496 tanks, 983 artillery pieces (including 452 l.FH18 105mm howitzers and 200 s.FH18 150mm guns), 473 81mm mortars and 800 anti-tank guns. Soviet losses in December were even heavier; the Western and Kalinin Fronts suffered 350,000 casualties – a 37 per cent casualty rate. Against the advice of Shaposhnikov and Zhukov, Stalin ordered the Stavka to plan a new, larger counteroffensive in January that was intended to encircle and destroy the bulk of Army Group Centre around Vyazma. The Soviet Counteroffensive during January–March 1942 put severe pressure on Army Group Centre across its front but failed to achieve its objectives.

Hitler was infuriated with the poor performance of his generals in failing to capture Moscow and particularly by their inability to stop the Soviet Winter Counteroffensive. Hitler's trust in the superiority of his generals' military skills was seriously reduced by the failure of Typhoon. He began by relieving Field Marshal von Brauchitsch as Commander-in-

A Soviet infantry unit, probably from one of the new rifle brigades, advances through a wooded area in December 1941. These troops appear well supplied with winter camouflage but have little in the way of support weapons. (Central Museum of the Armed Forces Moscow via Nik Cornish)

Chief of the army and Field Marshal von Bock on 19 December. During the next three weeks, three of the six army commanders (Guderian, Hoepner and Strauss) and four of the 22 corps commanders (Geyr von Schweppenburg, Förster, Geyer and Wäger) in Army Group Centre were relieved. Von Kluge took over Army Group Centre and Model took over Ninth Army. Although Guderian's adherents depicted his relief as unjustified, the fact is that twice he had allowed large Soviet forces to escape from encirclement and the performance of his army in Typhoon was sub-par. The removal of eight of 30 senior officers in Army Group Center was hardly a purge and, if anything, Hitler should be faulted for not going far enough. Von Kluge's disobedience on the Nara River had sabotaged Typhoon's last chance and Reinhardt's poor performance in the battle of the Klin Bulge almost resulted in the loss of four panzer divisions. On the positive side, Hitler began to usher out some of the older General Staff officers whom the OKH had preferred in favor of battlefield commanders, like Model, von Manteuffel and Eberbach. Hitler also rectified his mistaken reductions in armaments' production in mid-1941 and ordered major increases in weapons' production and the creation of new divisions. Furthermore, the Germans recognized the superiority of the Soviet T-34 tank and before Typhoon had even ended, development work had begun on the Tiger and Panther tank designs. Defeat in Typhoon left the Ostheer a wounded animal, but one that was beginning to prepare for a more intense campaign in 1942.

THE WEATHER FACTOR

The entire issue of the impact of poor weather conditions upon the conduct of Operation Typhoon has been distorted by decades of disinformation from both sides and gross oversimplification. Operation Typhoon was fought over a large area – 500km from north to south – and weather conditions often varied considerably along the front. It is clear from both German and Soviet weather data that while the offensive was hindered by passing periods of poor weather, that the worst winter weather did not arrive until after Typhoon had culminated. German weather data collected from all six armies involved in Typhoon demonstrate that the first snowfall, about 5cm in the period 7–13 October, fell mostly in the southern areas where Guderian was operating and did not effect Ninth Army, in the north around Rzhev, at all. Although the October snow melted quickly, it did not render every road impassable. On 10 October Fourth Panzer Army noted, 'here and there, the roads are hardly passable' and Guderian's own command recorded that 'motorized movement is partly impossible in some areas'. German records also indicate that the roads began drying out after four days and the mud phase in early October lasted for only about one week. Rain from 27 October to 3 November produced more mud, as well as a rainy period on 19–24 November, but in each case the effect of mud was fairly temporary and localized. It was never the case that all the roads in the AGC area were simultaneously impassable due to muddy conditions. The greatest impact of the mud upon German operations was to add further strain to the impoverished Wehrmacht logistical system.

The impact of cold weather upon ill-clad Wehrmacht troops has been cited as a primary factor in stopping Typhoon. In October, daytime

temperatures were mostly in the range 0° to 15° C (32–59° F), with frost on about one-third of the nights. It was coldest in the Third Panzer Army area around Rzhev. Temperatures did drop significantly in November, with daytime temperatures in the range 13° to 30° F and with frost on 80 per cent of nights. While the German front-line troops were certainly miserable in this cold, damp weather, temperatures in this range did not begin to cause significant amounts of illness and frostbite until the end of November, at which point Typhoon was already culminating from supply shortages. Snowfall in November was about 20cm and the freezing conditions actually improved German mobility. The terrible freezing temperatures and heavy snowfalls did not actually begin until 4 December, at which point Typhoon was over. During the onset of the Soviet Winter Counteroffensive, temperatures fell below 0° F from 4–7 December, which had a great impact upon the morale and health of the front-line German troops and helps to explain how the Soviets were able to achieve some of their breakthroughs. The intense cold drove German infantry indoors, allowing Soviet infantry and cavalry to infiltrate and envelop units that ceased to maintain continuous fronts. The worst freezing temperatures were around the Moskva–Volga Canal, which makes the Soviet breakthrough on the Klin Bulge more understandable. The weather did warm up during 8–12 December, which helped the Germans to mount a tenacious defense of Klin, but fell below 0° F again on 13–15 December. To sum up, the debilitating and casualty-inducing cold temperatures did not arrive until the point at which Typhoon had failed anyway, but this weather did assist the Soviet Counteroffensive.

CONCLUSION

The primary reasons that Operation Typhoon failed was serious German operational mistakes, combined with a logistic system that was not up to the task. The critical operational mistakes were: (1) Hitler and the OKH's failure to weight the main effort to seize Moscow, in that they

maintained simultaneous offensives in the other two army groups that deprived Army Group Centre of vital reinforcements and supplies, (2) Guderian failed to seal off the Bryansk and Trubchevsk Pockets, which allowed thousands of Soviet troops to escape to Tula, (3) the OKH's dilution of the main effort by directing Ninth Army and part of Third Panzer Army to advance northward towards Kalinin and Second Army to advance towards Kursk, (4) von Kluge's deliberate disobedience in not supporting the second phase of Typhoon, (5) von Bock's removal of virtually all of Third Panzer Army's infantry divisions in order to reinforce the operationally useless fighting around Kalinin, (6) Reinhardt's failure to maintain an adequate mobile reserve to safeguard his vulnerable left flank, (7) the diversion of Luftwaffe assets to other fronts just as Typhoon was approaching success deprived Army Group Centre of vital close air support, and (8) von Bock's operational plan for a double envelopment ignored the shortage of fuel, distances and terrain involved and weather constraints. In essence, Typhoon was a flawed plan, executed poorly and only initially successful due to the gross ineptitude of the Red Army.

Although the Soviets like to claim that they stopped the German offensive, the performance of the Red Army against Typhoon was generally weak. Despite the fact that the Western Front had established a fortified line with reserves, Army Group Centre penetrated the Soviet front line at multiple points and encircled the bulk of the Western and Bryansk Fronts in a week. Other than a few examples of small units putting up stout resistance, most Soviet units ran away or collapsed in front of the blitzkrieg. Boldin's defense of Tula was the only major Soviet defensive success during Typhoon.

THE BATTLEFIELD TODAY

Although there are a number of military tours in modern Russia that cater to those interested in Moscow and World War II, few go much beyond the outskirts of the capital. Anyone interested in visiting the actual battlefields of the Moscow campaign – since no fighting took place within Moscow proper – will have to design their own itinerary. Furthermore, most of the museums focusing on military history are centred in the capital, leaving little relevant to Operation Typhoon to see in places such as Klin, Kalinin, Mozhaisk or Tula.

Moscow does have a number of decent military museums either within the city or nearby that feature items pertinent to the defence of the capital in 1941. The most noteworthy museums are the Central Museum of the Great Patriotic War and the Central Armed Forces Museum. Although these museums have a large amount of World War II material, they are primarily geared to commemorating the victorious days of 1943–45, rather than the dark days of 1941. Other public memorials include the Defence of Moscow State Museum, the underground command centre of Stalin, Victory Square, the Tomb of the Unknown Soldier and the statue of Marshal Georgi Zhukov. At least two worthwhile Russian museums require special permission – the Air Defence History Museum and Military-Historical Museum of Armoured Vehicles and Equipment (aka the Kubinka Tank Museum). These museums emphasize equipment, particularly tanks and artillery displays and Kubinka is unique in having one of the largest historical tank inventories in the world.

Further afield, the battlefield of Borodino – although primarily focused on the 1812 campaign – does contain a number of World War II concrete bunkers, including some from the original Mozhaisk Line that the Germans breached in October 1941. The train from Belorus Station in Moscow takes about 2½ hours to reach Borodino station, making this probably the best day trip outside Moscow to view some of the terrain over which the campaign was decided. There are day trips available to Klin (which was heavily damaged in the war), Istra and Tula, but these are almost exclusively focused on cultural sites such as the Tchaikovsky and Tolstoy museums. For the adventurous, there is actually little of World War II interest to see in most of these areas, but on the plus side, the terrain in places like Mtensk and Yakhroma (which still has a steel bridge over the Moskva–Volga Canal, but not the original) has actually changed very little in the past 60 years and still remains essentially rural.

FURTHER READING

Armstrong, Richard N., *Red Army Tank Commanders: The Armored Guards*, Atglen, PA: Schiffer Military, 1994

Bergstrom, Christer, and Mikhailov, Andrey, *Black Cross/Red Star*, Vol. 1, Pacifica, CA: Pacifica Military History, 2000

Carell, Paul, *Hitler Moves East*, New York: Little Brown, 1964

Carell, Paul, *Operation Barbarossa in Photographs*, Atglen, PA: Schiffer Military, 1991

Chew, Allen F., *Fighting the Russians in Winter: Three Case Studies*, Leavenworth Paper 5, December, 1981

Creveld, Martin Van, *Supplying War*, London: Cambridge University Press, 1977

Erickson, John, *The Road to Stalingrad*, Boulder, CO: Westview Press, 1975

Glantz, David M., *A History of Soviet Airborne Forces*, Portland, OR: Frank Cass, 1994

Glantz, David M., *Barbarossa: Hitler's Invasion of Russia 1941*, Charleston, SC: Tempus Publishing, 2001

Glantz, David M., *Atlas of the Battle of Moscow: The Defensive Phase*, self-published, 1997

Guderian, Heinz, *Panzer Leader*, New York: Ballantine, 1957

Haupt, Werner, *Assault on Moscow 1941*, Atglen, PA: Schiffer Military History, 1996

Jentz, Thomas L. (ed.), *Panzertruppen, Germany's Tank Force, 1939–1942*, Vol. 1, Atglen, PA: Schiffer Military History, 1996.

Kahn, David, *Hitler's Spies: German Military Intelligence in World War II*, Cambridge, MA: Da Capo Press, 1978

Kershaw, Robert J., *War Without Garlands*, New York: Sarpedon, 2000

Krivosheev, Colonel General G. F., *Soviet Casualties and Combat Losses in the Twentieth Century*, Greenhill Books: London, 1997

Raus, Erhard, *Panzer Operations*, Cambridge, MA: Da Capo Press, 2003

Seaton, Albert. *The Battle for Moscow*, New York: Stein and Day, 1971

Zhukov, Georgi K., *Marshal Zhukov's Greatest Battles*, Harper & Row: New York, 1968

The Attack of the 44th Russian Cavalry Division at Musino, 17 November 1941, German intelligence report, T315, Roll 1246, Frame 682

Klima Des Ostlande (Climate of the Eastlands), Part I and II, Berlin: OKL (Luftwaffe) Study, 1944

INDEX

Figures in **bold** refer to illustrations

aircraft **36**
Akulovo 76
Aleksin 79
ammunition supplies 24, 71
artillery
  anti-aircraft **63–6**
  anti-tank 21, **22**, **27**, **43–4**, **64–6**, **86**
  German 21–2, **23**, **43**, **45**, **72–4**
  howitzers **23**, **72–4**
  losses 89
  mortars **45**
  rocket launchers **51**
  Soviet 26, 27, **44**, **51**, **63–7**, **72–4**, **83**,
    86
  USVs **83**

Bock, Field Marshal Fedor von **12**
  before campaign 7–8, 9, 11, 16
  campaign operations 30, 36, 43, 48, 49,
    61, 63, 70–1, 77, 79, 84, 86
  and campaign's failure 90, 92
Bogorodisk 85
Boldin, Lieutenant General Ivan V. **19**, 20,
  39, 42, 48, 79, 92
Borodino 49, 54, 56–7, 93
Bryansk 31, 37, 38–9, 42–3
Bryansk Pocket 31, 42–3, 48–9

cars **54**, **80–2**, **92**
casualties 49, 57, 89
Chern 59
clothing supplies 23, **58**, **89**
communications 26

Dedilovo 85

Eberbach, Colonel Heinrich 18, 44, 66
Essman 32

Fedorovka 86
fuel supplies 24, 43–4, 71, 78

German Army 21–5
  battle order 28
  competence 8
  panzer corps nomenclature 20
  personnel replacements 24–5
  Typhoon size and superiority 13
German Army units
  armies
    Second 31, 37, 43, 48, 55, 58, 59, 60,
      61–2, 70, 79–83, 88
    Fourth 37–8, 42, 48, 58, 61–2, 70, 76,
      77, 79, 85, 88
    Ninth 36–7, 39, 42, 48, 50, 55–6, 63,
      70, 75–7, 84, 85, 87
  battalions
    34th Motorcycle Infantry 33
    62nd Panzer Pioneer 76, **80–2**

corps
  V 36, 42, 48, 49, 57, 76, 77, 78
  VI 31, 36, 55
  VII 37, 42, 48
  VIII 37, 39, 42, 48
  IX 37, 42, 48, 76, 77, 85
  XII 34, 35, 55, 61–2
  XIII 31, 55, 58, 61–2, 79
  XX 37, 76, 79
  XXIII 55
  XXVII 37, 42, 48, 75–7, 85
  XXXIV 30, 58, 85, 88
  XXXV 30, 48, 58, 85
  XLIII 43, 55, 58, 59, 60, 61, 79–83
  LIII 37, 43, 58, 60–1, 79
divisions
  1st Cavalry 30, 48–9
  3rd Motorized 57
  10th Motorized Infantry 32, 60
  14th Motorized Infantry 35–6, 84–6, 87
  17th Infantry 62
  29th Motorized 48, 60, 83
  36th Motorized 84–6
  45th Infantry 88
  95th Infantry 88
  106th Infantry **72–4**, 76
  112th Infantry 48, 60
  129th Infantry 35–6
  134th Infantry 88
  258th Infantry 61
  296th Infantry 60
  SS Reich 31, **49**, 51–4, 56–7, 76, 78,
    85, 86
Kampfgruppe Eberbach 32, 33, 41,
  44–8, 57, 59, 60, **64–6**, 79–83
Lehr 900 Motorized Brigade 55
panzer armies/groups
  2nd 7, 12, 30–3, 43–8, 58, 59–61,
    64–6, 70, 79–83, 85, 87–8
  3rd 7, 12, 31, 35–6, 50, 55–6, 63, 70,
    75–8, 84, 85, 86–7
  4th 12, 13, 31, 34–5, 40, 51–4, 55,
    56–7, 61–2, 70, 76, 77, 86, 87
panzer corps
  XXIV 30–2, 33, 43, 59–60, **64–6**,
    79–83, 85, 88
  XL 31, 34–5, 41, 48, 51–4, 56–7, 70,
    76, 77, 78, 87
  XLI 35–6, 41, 56, 63, 87
  XLVI 34, 35, 48, 57, 70, 76, 77, 78
  XLVII 30, 31, 32, 33, 38, 43, 49, 60,
    79, 88
  XLVIII 30, 32, 43, 48, 59
  LVI 35–6, 39, 48, 76, 77, 78, 86, 87
  LVII 34, 35, 55, 57, 76, 79
panzer divisions
  1st 31, 35–6, 55–6, 63, 87
  2nd 34–5, 67, 76, 77, 78, 86, 87
  3rd 32, 44, 59, 60, **64–6**, 79–83
  4th 32, 33, 43–8, 59, 60, 79–83
  5th 34, 35, 77

6th 35–6, 39, 86, 87
7th 35–6, 39, 41, 42, 76, 87
10th 31, 34–5, 42, 51–4, 56–7, 76, 87
11th 34, 77
17th 42–3, 60, 79–83
18th 43, 48
19th 57
20th 57, 79
regiments
  35th Panzer 33
  107th Artillery **72–4**
  Der Führer 51
  Grossdeutschland 60, **64–6**, 83
Geyr von Schweppenburg, General Leo
  Baron 18, 33, 45, 59, 90
Gorodniansky, Major General Avksentii 33
Guderian, Colonel General Heinz **16**
  before campaign 7–8, 9, 11, 16, 17
  campaign operations 30–3, 43–50,
    59–61, 79–83, 85, 87–8
  and campaign's failure 90, 92
Gzhatzk 31, 51

Halder, Colonel General Franz 11, 50
halftracks **50**, **64–6**
Hausser, Obergruppenführer Paul 51–4, 56
Hitler, Adolf **12**
  before campaign 8, 9, 11–12
  and campaign operations 50, 63–7, 84,
    89–90, 91–2
  conspiracy against 17
Hoepner, Colonel General Erich 16–17,
  34–5, 77–8, 87, 90
Hoth, Colonel General Hermann 9, 35–6

Istra 76, 77, 78, 85, 86–7, 93

Kalinin 31, 50, 55–6, 63, 70, 75–7, 84,
  85, 87
Kaluga 31, 55, 89
Karachev 31
Katukov, Colonel Mikhail E. 20, 41, 44–5
Keitel, Field Marshal Wilhelm 11
Kesselring, Field Marshal Albert 9
Khimki 76, **80–2**
Kholm-Zhirkovski 36, 39
Kiev 8–9, 13
Kirov 40
Klin 76, 77–8, 93
Klin Bulge 84–7
Kluge, Field Marshal Günther von **17**
  before campaign 16, 17
  campaign operations 38–9, 56, 61–2, 76,
    79, 92
  promoted 90
Kolomna 70
Konev, Colonel General Ivan **18**
  background and experience 19
  campaign operations 39, 41, 42, 48, 63,
    84, 85
  and Stalin 18, 19, 40

Krasnaya Polyana 76, 78, 86
Kromy 31, 33
Kubelwagens **80–2**
Kursk 48, 59

Lama River 76, 77
Lelyushenko, Major General Dmitri
    Danilovich **20**
    background and experience 20
    campaign operations 38, 41, 45, 54,
        56–7, 59, 77–8, 85–7
Lemelsen, General Joachim 18, 33
Leningrad 8, 9, 13, 19
Livny 88
Lobnya 76
logistics 13, 23–4, **24–5**, 34, **34**, **40**, 43–4,
    58, 70–1
Luftwaffe 22–3, 32, 34, 36, 45, 63, 70

Maloyaroslavets 57
Manteuffel, Colonel Hasso von 18, 41, 78
Medyn 55
Mikhailov 85, 88
military intelligence 13, 15
Minsk Pocket 7
Model, Colonel General Walther 18, 35–6,
    63, 90
Moscow
    axis dispositions, 30 September **14**
    defences round 13–15, 27
    desirability as objective 9, 11–12
    militia **62**
Moscow campaign: maps **6**, **31**, **76**, **85**
Moscow Sea 75–7
Moskva River 63
motorcycles **80–2**
Mozhaisk Line 31, 42, 51–4, 56–7
Mtensk 31, 40, 41, 45–8, 59, 85, 93
Musino **72–4**

Nara River 61–2, 76, 79
Naro-Fominsk 61, 76, 79

Orel 31, 33, **36**, 40–1

Pavlov, General 7, 40
Peshki 78
Petrov, Major General Mikhail 48
Plavsk 59

railways and railheads 23–4, 26, 71
Reinhardt, Colonel General Hans Georg
    16, 17, 78, 84–7, 90, 92
road conditions **25**, **37**, **40**, **54**, **59**
Rogachevo 76, 78
Rokossovsky, Major General Konstantin
    19–20, **19**, 57, 75–9, 86, 87
Rotmistrov, Colonel Pavel A. 20, 86, 87
Rzhev 31, 49, 50, 55, 89

Schaal, General Ferdinand 86, 87
Sevsk 31, 32–3
Shaposhnikov, Marshal Boris 13, **13**, 18, 42,
    50, 51, 57, 84
Smolensk 7–8, 9, 19
Sobennikov, Lieutenant General Petr 34,
    35
Solnechnogorsk 76, 78, 85, 87
Soviet Air Force (VVS) 25, 26, 27, 36, 70
Soviet Army 25–7
    battle order 29
    cavalry **91**

guards units 26
prisoners **42**
Siberian units 27, 60, 67, 76, 78, 79
ski battalions **75**
Soviet Army units
    armies
        1st Shock 76, 78, 84, 85, 86
        3rd 31, 43, 48–9, 60–1, 88
        5th 54, 56–7, 61, 63, 67, 76, 79, 85, 87
        10th 84, 85, 88
        13th 31, 33, 38, 43, 48–9, 85, 88
        16th 37, 41, 42, 48, 56, 57, 63, 67, 70,
            72–4, 76, 77, 85, 86
        19th 35–6, 37, 39, 41, 42, 48
        20th 37–8, 41, 42, 48, 76, 84, 85, 86
        22nd 49–50, 55, 63
        24th 37–8, 42
        29th 49–50, 55, 63, 85
        30th 31, 35–6, 39, 55, 75–7, 84–7
        31st 55, 63, 84, 85
        32nd 41, 42, 48
        33rd 31, 35, 57, 61, 76, 79
        43rd 31, 34–5, 37, 56, 57, 61
        49th 61
        50th 31, 37, 43, 48, 61, 79–83, 85, 88
    Bryansk Front 9, 13, 30–3, 37, 38–9,
        42–3, 48–9
    corps
        1st Guard Cavalry 85, 88
        1st Guard Rifle 40
        2nd Guard Cavalry 85, 87
        5th Airborne 40–1
    divisions
        1st NKVD Special Motorized **61**
        44th Cavalry **72–4**
    Dovator's Cavalry Group 13–15, 39,
        49–50, 85, 87
    Group Belov 85
    Kalinin Front 63, 67, 77–8, 85, 89
    Operational Group Ermakov 30–3
    regiments
        2nd Motorized 87
        46th Motorcycle 87
        132nd NKVD Border Guard 40–1
    Reserve Front 13, 31, 34–5, 38, 39–40,
        48–50, 51
    rifle divisions
        1st Guards Motorized 61
        5th Guards 41
        6th Guards 41
        32nd 49, 54, 56–7
        53rd 34–5
        78th Siberian 76, 78
        82nd Motorized 57
        91st 35
        149th 34–5
        162nd 35–6
        283rd 32
        290th 60
        298th 33
        312th 56
        316th 56, 57
        413th Siberian 60, 79
    Southwest Front 85, 88
    tank brigades
        4th 41, 57, 59
        8th 86, 87
        11th 41
        18th 51–4
        19th 51–4
        20th 57
        21st 87

32nd 59
121st 32
141st 33
143rd 39
145th 35, 38
146th 78
148th 35
150th 32
tank divisions: 108th 37
Western Front 9, 13–15, 31, 35–6, 37–8,
    39, 40–2, 48–50, 51, 55–6, 58, 67,
    71–5, 89
Spas-Demensk 40, 41
Stalin, Joseph **61**
    before campaign 7, 9, 13, 15
    and campaign operations 38, 40, 42, 75,
        84, 89
    and Konev 18, 19, 40
Stalinogorsk 85
Stavka
    before campaign 9, 13, 15, 26, 27
    and campaign operations 31, 38, 40, 41,
        54, 75
Strauss, Colonel General Adolf 17, 36–7,
    90
Stumme, General Georg 18, 56, 78
Sukhinici 55

tanker trucks **24**
tanks
    German 21, **22**, **32**, **34**, **54**, **64–6**, 90
    Soviet 25–6, **27**, **33**, 35, **62**, **70–4**, **77**, 78
Teploye 60–1
Timoshenko, Marshal 7, 85, 88
Trubchevsk Pocket 31, 43, 48–9
trucks **24**, **37**, **59**
Tula 59–61, **60**, **64–6**, 70, 79–83, 88, 93

Uzlovaia 79

Venev 85
Volokolamsk 57
VVS see Soviet Air Force
Vyazma 31, 34, 35, 89
Vyazma Pocket 31, 41–2, 48, 49

weapons
    German 21
    hand grenades **8**
    machine guns **38–9**, **55**
    machine pistols **30**
    Soviet 25–6, **55**
    see also artillery
weather 90–1
Weichs, Colonel General Maximilian von
    17–18, **17**, 37, 43

Yakhroma 76, 78, 93
Yartsevo 37
Yefrimov 85
Yelets 85
Yelnya 8, 9, 19, 37–8, 54, 56
Yepifan 60, 61
Yeremenko, Lieutenant General Andrei 9,
    13, 19, 32, 38–9, 43
Yukhnov 40, 42

Zhukov, General Georgi **18**
    before campaign 9, 18–19
    campaign operations 40, 42, 51, 56, 58,
        67, 71–5, 77, 79, 84, 85
Zusha River 59